Praise for *More than Gold*

"Bryan Elliott's book, *More Than Gold*, is a must read if you want to wake up every morning with a sense of expectation as to what God has in store for you. Bryan shows in practical ways, and using personal examples from his walk with God, how to take the power and the presence of God to your spheres of influence, particularly to the marketplace where we spend the bulk of our time. Get ready to be transformed so you can make the world a better place!"
—**Dr. Ed Silvoso,** Founder and President of Transform Our World Network

"What a power packed book! You have Bryan's compelling story interwoven with a compact, life-giving version of the gospels. These, plus the inside story of how God intervenes and redeems in human history, will bring revelation that draws you closer to God's Heart. And most importantly, you will learn what this means for YOU. Yes, YOU dear Reader. If you are already very secure in your salvation, you will get how to more fully engage in your Christian walk in an exciting authentic way. Otherwise, you can allow Bryan's journey both to challenge you and to boost you along your journey. Your bonus will be to know Father God in a very personal way. God is calling you into a fresh, dynamic, loving relationship worth more than gold."
—**Chester and Betsy Kylstra,** Founders of Restoring the Foundations International, RTF Healing House Network, and Transforming Your Business Network

"With refreshing vulnerability, Bryan shares his story and what God has taught him along the way. The lessons contained, if applied, will change lives. The dramatic transformation of both Bryan and his daughter, Bryn, is a testament to the truths written in this work. May all who read it be encountered by the God of all power and love even as they have been."

—**Patricia Bootsma,** Co-Outreach Director of Catch the Fire USA, Author of *Convergence, Raising Burning Hearts* and *A Lifestyle of Divine Encounters*

"This book was written for you... for every seeker, for every doubter, for every leader, for every believer! Bryan has masterfully interwoven practical steps to journey deeper with God. With raw passion, he authentically shares the pitfalls of his own life, from financial success to unimaginable tragedy. Be prepared to journey towards transformative freedom as you digest the message Bryan clearly and unashamedly shares: 'I know Jesus and want others to know Him because He has powerfully transformed my life.'"

—**Michael D. Pierce,** Executive Director, Christ For Your City

"Over the years I have learned that there are many who 'talk the talk' but far fewer who 'walk the walk'. Bryan Elliot is a man who truly 'walks the walk'. In his book, *More Than Gold*, he shares humbly, transparently, and powerfully about his journey and the lessons God has taught him along the way. As you read it, you will be challenged, convicted, encouraged, and inspired. Get ready to draw closer to God. Get ready to grow. Get ready for personal transformation. What God has done in Bryan's life, and the life of his daughter Bryn, is truly miraculous. I'm excited to see the miracles that manifest in the lives of those who read and put into practice the truths contained in this power packed book."

—**Brendan Witton,** Lead Pastor, Toronto City Church

REFLECTIONS ON

MORE THAN GOLD

LIVING IN GLORIOUS FREEDOM

BRYAN ELLIOTT

Cover by Allison Morris

Edited by Jessica Glasner and Allison Morris

ISBN: 979-8-9860882-2-8

Printed in the USA

First Edition

www.m46ministries.com

@M46Ministries

Contents

Part Two
Experiencing God

Part Three
Abiding in Christ

Part Four
Suffering for the Believer

Foreword I

Bryn S. Elliott

It is not a coincidence that you picked up this book. Jesus is pursuing your heart and right now He is standing on the other side of a wide-open door, inviting you into a relationship with Him. The relationship He offers is not like any you have experienced in the past. A relationship with Him will exceed your wildest expectations and really is *more valuable than gold*. It is a relationship that will fulfill the longings of your heart, bringing healing and restoration to the parts of you that are broken and hurting.

This book is the best tool I have ever come across to guide you into a real, authentic relationship with Jesus. Reading this book has brought a fresh fire to my walk with Jesus as I continue to realize that there is always more! This book is real and raw, telling the story of a man (my dad) who was broken and lost, but by the grace and power of God is now unashamed, unshackled, and a force for the Kingdom of light.

My dad shared the tools in this book with me little by little, as the Holy Spirit led Him. In doing so, my life was forever changed. In fact, my life was *literally* saved because of my dad's burning heart for Jesus. My dad lives a life of divine freedom and full surrender. The joy of the Lord radiates through him regardless of his circumstances. He truly lives his life at the feet of Jesus and it is my joy and honour to be able to walk with Jesus with my dad by my side. This is the greatest blessing my dad could ever give me as a daughter.

More than Gold was written for me... but it is now available to you, because God wants to do for you what He did in my life and in my dad's. He wants to set you free.

I hope that you can see and acknowledge that this book was written to be in your hands, that it is God's will is for you to know Him. He wants a deep, intimate relationship with you, and He is already waiting for you with open arms.

I can promise you from personal experience that the words contained in this book will lead you into deeper intimacy with God, healing, and freedom. Each page is packed with truth, wisdom and revelation. I encourage you to invite the Lord into your time reading. Allow Him to speak and make each section personal to your life. Spend time meditating on the scriptures woven throughout each page. The Word of God is active and living, and He is mighty to save!

God is inviting you to go deeper with Him, but it's your choice to accept His invitation. It is my prayer that you say *yes*, and dive into the glorious freedom He has waiting for you on the other side.

Bryn S. Elliott
Co-founder of M46 Ministries
Author of *Dying to Live*

Foreword II
Kenneth S. Gill

More Than Gold by Bryan Elliott reveals the power of testimony woven into a dynamic instrument on discipleship.

I see three things intricately intertwined throughout its pages: the power of the Spirit, the power of the Scriptures, and the power of Story. They are inextricably knit together to form a solid foundation for spiritual growth and ongoing development.

Upon writing this introduction, the price of gold in North America has been trending around the $2000.00 per ounce. Bryan's bold statement 'more than gold' references his journey of faith, highlighting the combined work of the Holy Spirit and Scripture to bring about continuous life-change. The value he places upon his faith journey is worth ... 'more than gold.' Think of that – more than history's value on this precious metal, gold as a highly valued commodity, he says his journey is worth *More Than Gold*.

As a disciple-maker for over 50 years, I have combed through scores of discipleship manuals and material throughout my life. As I embarked upon the adventure of reading through *More Than Gold*, I noted something unique to this writing. It seemed to be a relationally based discipleship tool. It was incredibly personal. The power of testimony captivated my heart. I could connect with him on a deeper level, identifying in his brokenness, the humility and vulnerability he experienced in turning his life over to the master discipler, Jesus. *More Than Gold* is a series of past and current life lessons from the author's life journey woven beautifully into a step-by-step unfolding of a new believer's journey in Christ.

Relationally-based, personal study discipleship tools are rarely found. Most discipleship tools are instructive, built on fundamental objective scriptural principles designed to take a new believer from 'here to there' beginning with 'milk principles' and the intention of moving towards 'meat principles,' as the new believer's maturation sojourn unfolds. The author, in this case, weaves masterfully the relational and the instructive to make this instrument a valuable tool.

The author esteems the centrality of the scriptures and their accurate application as 'more than gold.' This is very important as every believer's 'born again' experience begins with the' imperishable seed' of the Word of God taking root in our spirit, bringing about a similar transformation to which Bryan and his daughter, Bryn, experienced. To this experience, the author invites keen persons wanting to grow in their understanding of the Christian faith.

This written instrument lays out for the reader the beautiful latticework of the Holy Spirit's involvement in every step of our growth. The author conveys his trust in the leadership of the Holy Spirit and the importance of godly counsel and provides an invitation to enjoy true fellowship in a community of believers. I noted throughout the book the use of a constructive thought sequence that was highlighted either by design or default. Every chapter invites us to further reading opportunities, with the siting of book references, prayers that we can pray, and the posturing of pertinent questions following each teaching segment with encouragement to additional study and reflection.

Unique to this writing is the author's use of a quality self-reflection tool at the start and end of the book. I had not seen this implemented in the disciple-making process before. After giving ourselves an honest appraisal, we begin the adventure of exploring the life of faith in Christ. Upon concluding my study, I assess myself again to measure my progress. I believe this is a thoughtful and insightful gesture provided by the author to evaluate ourselves without anyone looking. This process invites the maturing Jesus follower to a life of continuous improvement with the assistance of The Spirit + The Word + a life connected to a community of believers.

To sum up my thoughts, the author, in this writing, interlinks in a practical sense the merger of a guidebook, a handbook, a workbook, a schoolbook, a reference book, and ultimately a cookbook. If you collect the broad nature of the subject matter covered, the personal nature of Bryan's testimony, the life-lessons, the work of the Holy Spirit, the full application of Scripture, and thoroughly mix the diversity of these ingredients, allowing them to simmer in our spirit, it will certainly provide a 'pure gold recipe' for maturity and a 'well balanced diet' for continual emotional and spiritual growth while offering to each disciple a vibrant spirituality when practised. Now, let's get on with the journey... and accept the author's invitation to live in *glorious freedom*.

Kenneth S. Gill
Ripple Cluster Apostolic Leader
Calgary, Alberta, Canada

To my mom,

Thank you for being unwavering in your faith, standing strong year after year in the midst of great trauma and personal loss. I will always be grateful for your strength, love, bravery, and steadfast prayers. I'm looking forward to writing our new story together.

Prologue

Brothers and sisters, we do not want you to be uninformed about those who sleep in death, so that you do not grieve like the rest of mankind, who have no hope.

—I Thessalonians 4:13

Everyone has experienced tragedy, suffering, and periods of doubt. Knowing Jesus doesn't mean you'll never experience pain, but rather, when you go through great periods of hardship, you will come out with the joy and strength of the Lord on the other side. It means you can face a firing squad, a life-threatening diagnosis, or an unthinkable tragedy and still hold on to the joy of your salvation.

There is glorious freedom awaiting everyone who turns to Jesus.

I hope believers new and old find encouragement and revelation in my story, though you should know I originally intended these words for my daughter, Bryn. The tragic loss of her sister, Abbe, awakened me to my calling as a father to teach, train, and spur my daughter on in the ways of the Lord. I began by writing about the gospel of grace as an anchor for her faith. Then I thought about her friends who didn't know the Lord, which inspired the next few sections. My love of practicing discipleship and a burning desire to share what God had done in my life continued to fuel my writing. I was so excited to share the goodness of God and the truth of the gospel, I literally could not stop writing, leading to multiple books including *More Than Gold*.

All are welcome to join the family of believers. God invites those who have experienced great suffering to lean on Him for comfort. He is a good God who desires good things for His children. However, in order to experience the goodness and the freedom He offers, we need to A) see Him rightly and B) believe rightly. God isn't distant and far off; He is with us and for us! As we come to know the truth of who God is and who we are, we bring heaven to earth in the here and now.

The Bible tells us that there is peace promised to those who put their trust in Jesus. It is a peace that surpasses all understanding. It is a peace unlike anything else found in this world because He is the Prince of Peace.

I've experienced this peace in the midst of the most difficult seasons of my life, and I've written the words in this book as a testimony of God's great love. In fact, the majority of this book was written during the Covid-19 pandemic in Canada under intense lockdown, with a murder trial, a divorce, the sale of our family home, and a lawsuit all running in parallel. In the midst of it all, I discovered that God is my source and through Him, I can live above my circumstances and thrive no matter what I may be facing. I discovered His love. A love that is merciful and just. A love that brings comfort, which pales in comparison to anything the world has to offer. A love that redeems and makes all things new. A love that brings glorious freedom!

What began as a father's simple way to share what he'd learnt with his daughter soon became something so much more. The reflections in this book were written to be read daily, though it may prove helpful for some to digest larger portions of the writings at a time. Be sensitive to the Holy Spirit, and read at the pace He directs. We are all on unique journeys. God will meet us where we are at, wherever that may be.

As you read, I hope that you benefit from what I've learnt, although I am by no means finished with my journey with the Lord. My goal is simply to present the basic concepts of what it means to believe in Jesus and enter a relationship with Him. The choice is yours. Your journey is your own. In the pages ahead, I pray that you will see yourself more clearly and understand God more fully because of the work He is already doing.

Introduction

Bryan Elliott

Before you dive into this journey of the theological foundations and spiritual disciplines that enabled me to walk with God and grow in faith, I want to share my own journey to the cross and the glorious freedom I experienced at the feet of Jesus.

May 23, 2018, started like any other day. It was a beautiful, sunny afternoon, and I was planning on leaving the office early when I received a call from the police. My daughter, Abbe, had been stabbed.

Assuming it was a minor incident, I immediately drove to Abbe's apartment, only to discover the entire street had been closed off. Police cars and ambulances had parked outside, and people rushed back and forth in a chaotic scene. A wave of disbelief washed over me. *What was happening to my family?*

After what seemed like an eternity, someone offered to drive me to the hospital. The drive was a blur.

I remember Abbe's mother calling to tell me she heard on the radio a woman had been stabbed and rushed to Sunnybrook Hospital with life-threatening injuries. Oddly, this was more than the police had told me on the scene, and I began to grasp the reality of the situation.

Over the next hour in the hospital waiting room, I experienced a host of conflicting feelings. Heaviness, sadness, disbelief, hope... emotions overlapped, started, and stopped at strange intervals. I didn't know what to think or feel. No one would tell our family or me what was going on. There was no follow-up explanation. The only direct information we had was from that first call telling us Abbe had been stabbed.

Family members arrived, one after another, gathering in silence as we waited for someone to tell us what was happening. When that moment finally came, the news was nearly impossible to believe. The doctors pronounced Abbe dead on arrival. The cause? She experienced five slash and stab knife wounds, with a stab wound to the heart as the ultimate cause of her death.

Everyone in the room cried out in sorrow and disbelief as the doctor's news sank in. I looked over and saw my younger daughter, Bryn, unravelling. Abbe was not just Bryn's only sister; she was her best friend. With my eyes locked on Bryn, my body registered severe, deep grief and debilitating disappointment.

Could this really be happening? If it is, how could God allow it?

My daughter had been stabbed in the heart. It was unimaginable. A tragic ending for my beautiful baby girl. Only 21 years old. Abbe had tried and tried to get back on her feet from a life marked by intense suffering, tragedy, and ongoing struggles. After giving her life to the Lord and unsuccessfully attempting to heal from years of drug addiction and trauma, *how could it end like this? How could something this terrible happen?*

The Unexplainable in the Face of the Unspeakable

After hours of crying and trying to absorb what had happened, I went to bed that night, exhausted and numb. There was a void in my soul, the feeling that something precious was ripped from me. My mind raced. Heaviness filled my heart as I thought about my traumatized family and how Abbe was gone forever. Our lives would never be the same.

Yet, unexpectedly, I woke the next morning with an incredible and unexplainable peace I attribute solely to the grace of God. I was overwhelmed by the revelation that Abbe was in heaven with the Lord. She was now safe for all eternity with her Father in heaven, His great mercy revealed in her life.

A true revelation and the experience of His mercy had produced in me a tangible joy, despite the devastating tragedy that had befallen my family. In His sovereignty, God saw the end from the beginning and He allowed me to feel the heavenly reality that Abbe was finally home, safe and sound.

Very few could understand what I was experiencing. In fact, many told me I was in denial, while others accused me of suppressing my pain. I even received a third-party diagnosis that I had disassociated from the trauma of what had happened.

I can see how others may have seen my unexplainable peace and joy as insensitive. We were all mourning the loss of Abbe; many of those dearest to my heart were sinking in the grief of her death. Some even resented and judged me, not understanding how God could possibly give me joy in the midst of such a grievous loss.

My family suffered severe shock and trauma after Abbe's death. Yet, I also knew God was depositing something different in me. It was a feeling of peace so exceptionally significant that it would direct the next part of my journey in ways I'd never expect. He was doing the unexplainable in the midst of the unspeakable.

Looking Back

Looking back over my life, I am confident that the profound power and presence of God I experienced in the season of Abbe's loss wasn't an isolated incident. Rather, it was the fruit of what God had been cultivating in my life for several years.

As someone who grew up going to church, my relationship with Jesus had become lukewarm at best. I never questioned the validity of Christianity. I came from generations of Christians and found the evidence surrounding Jesus' deity, death, and resurrection compelling and believed that Jesus was the Messiah... but I didn't know Him personally.

I also experienced a great tragedy when I was just 14 years old when a devastating gun accident left my brother in a vegetative state. In the following years, I watched our family dissolve in resentment, shame, and unprocessed grief. My dad became dependent on alcohol and left my mom after he lost his business. My other brother struggled for years, attempting suicide multiple times.

By the age of 18, I had become disillusioned with the Church. I had built up arguments and offenses that were really just excuses to live life on my own terms. I figured I would become a Christian again one day—after I had had my fun and lived life on my terms. As a result, I left the Church completely for more than a decade but eventually made my way back, inch by inch, until 2016, when I truly made Jesus Lord of my life. Before then, my relationship with Jesus was nominal. I considered myself a good person, but this belief only gave me a thin and false sense of peace and righteousness based on my own merits.

In the interim, I married my daughters' mother (my first marriage). She was my university sweetheart, but she had a lot of personal troubles that led her to leave me when the girls were still toddlers. I had other relationships with women that were damaging to my daughters after their mother left. I even allowed someone to become close to our family who was, unknown to me, abusive to my girls in the worst possible ways. This would ultimately lead to years of addiction and mental health struggles for both of my girls.

I married again when the girls were in their pre-teens, and for the third time when the girls were teens. My third wife was kind and stable, the kind of woman I thought would help bring a sense of order back to my home. She was not a believer, although she was fine with me being a (lukewarm) believer as I was when we first moved in together in 2012. Ultimately, we had mistakenly rushed our relationship, the damage to my girls was done, and the many years of trauma we experienced took a deep toll on both her and the marriage.

Turning Point

In December 2015, two and a half years before Abbe's death, God connected me to a wonderful group of believers in Saint John, New Brunswick. Little did I know that this connection would become the impetus for me to go after Jesus wholeheartedly for the first time in my life.

It was with this group of passionate Christians that I tasted the glorious freedom that comes from knowing Jesus personally. Everything from that point on changed, and my life would never be the same, nor did I want it to be.

The community I found was incredibly patient with my journey and they even started a weekly prayer group to pray for me and my business. I discovered and began applying biblical priorities to my life, putting God at the top of my list, followed by my family, business, church, and friends. As the months passed and I saw their authentic and passionate love for God and for people, I knew I needed to do more. Sowing donations into their ministry and paying a full-time inter-cessor or having a prayer team wasn't enough. God wanted me to do my own praying!

I had always been afraid of praying out loud, especially in front of a group of people. If I did pray out loud, it was only to recite the Lord's Prayer. But as this community led me into deeper encounters with the Word of God, I couldn't help but want to grow in this area.

Up to this point, I had enjoyed the finest things life had to offer without restraint: NBA courtside season tickets, luxurious vacations, expensive nights out, engaged in the foothills of the Andes in a vineyard in Argentina, married on a 900-acre estate in Tuscany, living in a six-million-dollar house, an expensive wine collection, etc.

Even though I had been both successful and generous, I found my secu-rity in wealth. What's more, I was very undisciplined and a poor steward of the resources He had given me to manage. My personal finances needed tightening. My business had areas that were not in order. My giving needed discipline. In short, my bucket had holes and was leaking. Essentially, God wanted full disclosure of my accounts, so He could lead me into greater surrender and obedience. I needed His wisdom.

Learning to pray launched something entirely new in my life, family, business, and beyond. I discovered just how much I needed to show up in my own relationship with God. Nobody else could do it for me. If I wanted to know God, *I needed to do it for myself.*

The Next Layer

Eager to develop my relationship with God, I dove into the Word and the process of inner healing. He set me free from various strongholds that had held me in bondage for years. My views on praying in tongues even changed as my engineer brain began to give way to my heart which was being strengthened in the Holy Spirit daily.

God was more concerned with my heart than allowing me to continue believing the lies buried deep within me. As such, He began to pull away the things I had leaned on for strength separate from Him. My business began to shake, I lost millions in key investments, and even though we were now praying two times a week for my business, things just kept getting worse. To compound matters, my daughters were continuing to spiral down into addiction, ultimately leading to the tragic loss of my oldest daughter, Abbe.

There is no way I could have mustered up the peace and joy I experienced directly following Abbe's death on my own. It was only by God's grace, stemming from a deep awareness that Abbe was securely resting in her eternal home in heaven. This awareness was the result of the fresh relationship with Jesus I had been cultivating in the secret place since deciding to surrender my life to Him completely, from the inside out. Grounding my trust in the goodness, faithfulness, and mercy of God allowed me to keep my heart soft.

By God's Grace Alone

Even when Your path takes me through the valley of deepest darkness, fear will never conquer me, for You already have!

Your authority is my strength and my peace. The comfort of Your love takes away my fear. I'll never be lonely, for You are near.

—Psalm 23:4, TPT

Prior to Abbe's death, I had already planned on hosting our prayer group in my downtown Toronto office for a week of 24/7 prayer over the upcoming elections. The director of the group came early and arrived just days after we lost Abbe (New Brunswick to Ontario is a long trek). He and a few others interceded and held me up for a full week after the funeral.

My family of believers understood the peace and joy God had given me, where many others could not. Even when I became weak, and torment began to overshadow my heart, they gathered and began praying Psalm 23 over me. This immediately restored my sense of peace, and I fell asleep right there in my office.

I had to process Abbe's death. We all did. But I never doubted that God had my daughter. The unwavering sense of peace and joy, knowing Abbe was home, never left me, and it stayed with me as life marched on, applying itself to new trials and moments of pain. At times, I had to be careful how I demonstrated this powerful overflow of the presence of God. Filled with unexplainable joy and gratitude, I remember choosing to walk alone to and from the funeral parlour because I couldn't help but sing the song God had put on my heart at the top of my lungs, over and over:

> *"For His name is glorious, glorious, glorious*
> *Make His praise glorious, glorious, glorious*
> *Shout His name Glorious, Glorious, Glorious."* [1]

Through the Valley of the Shadow of Death

Abbe's funeral was held at my local church. I led the 90-minute service, and my pastor delivered a short message. Despite the circumstances, I was determined to continue believing in God's goodness and wanted to give Him glory. It was a powerful, praise-filled celebration of life, one fraught with pain and unspeakable suffering, but not one without a few bright spots.

Family, friends, business leaders, drug dealers, gang members, and pastors, probably more unbelievers than believers, all came to say goodbye to Abbe. We expected a small turnout, but the number of people who showed up overwhelmed us. Over 400 people came to celebrate Abbe's life with us, so many that the crowd even spilled into the church lobby.

In spite of the great mourning that day, many shared stories of how Abbe had helped friends and even saved lives because of her actions. Over and over, people described her as someone who was there for them in the darkest period of their lives when no one else was.

Everyone who came that day heard the gospel and experienced (maybe for the first time) the incredible hope that we have as Christians.

Through Crystal's Eyes

Walking into the church, I could feel the depths of despair hovering over the crowded room. Everyone was mourning the loss of their beloved Abbe. While standing at the back of the crowd, I watched Bryn, Abbe's sister, sob her way through her tribute to her beautiful older sister. Abbe's death happened so quickly and was devastating. It was an unexpected blow. Yet, in the midst of so much grief, Bryan stepped on the platform radiating light from within, consistently communicating that Jesus gives all of us hope. All of us.

There were many others who spoke after Bryan, encouraging those to anchor their frail hearts to a real Jesus. As a follower of Christ, tears welled up in my eyes watching this beautiful oxymoron of messages unfold. One thing remained: the radiant truth of Jesus' love. It provided hope beyond this temporal life in the midst of such sorrow. God's love for humanity is real and available to all who reach for Him.

—Crystal Lavallee, family friend

A Peace That Surpasses All Understanding

Since Abbe went home to heaven, I've faced difficult relationship challenges, including life-and-death situations with my only other daughter, Bryn. I've had multi-million dollar business deals go sideways. I've been in lawsuits. I lost my marriage and my house. Abbe's murder trial went on for years. And yet God's abiding peace continues in my life. His love continues to hold me up and stabilise me through storms past and present.

I'm not the only one who has experienced this incredible peace and joy in the midst of a situation that could easily leave a person physically, mentally, and emotionally devastated.

At a Christian conference in San Jose, California, hosted by *Transform Our World*, I shared my story in front of a room of about a thousand people. To my surprise, many who had experienced unimaginable losses and tragedies came up to me afterwards to share that they, too, had had similar experiences with God in the darkest periods of their lives. It was as though there was a special band of brothers and sisters bound together by the joy of the Lord in their suffering, and I was suddenly a member.

So why am I telling you this? Supernatural empowerment is meant to be the norm for the Body of Christ.

And for those who don't know Jesus, you're invited to be set gloriously free from the chains that bind us on this earth. In the midst of great sadness and pain (and celebration, too!), God wants us to know Him and live in the fullness of all He has for us. His gifts of mercy and love are waiting for us if only we surrender our lives to Him.

My purpose on this earth is to worship God and bring Him glory. He has called me to lead others to the glorious freedom I have experienced through knowing Him, which is how this book came to be. These reflections started as my story of knowing God and being sanctified through the pursuit of His Word resulting in glorious freedom. *More Than Gold* is a testimony that God's love can triumph over any challenge and bring you into a place of stability and victory in Him!

Just a few short years ago, my life looked nothing like Christ's. Failed marriages, ungodly relationships, and an aborted first child filled my history. I had poor boundaries as a parent. I selfishly and quickly moved my girls into new relationships and living arrangements. I was self-focused, self-indulgent, and self-serving (and blind to it). Generosity was a value I espoused, however, glorifying God was not my primary motive. I gave more out of fear or trying to earn God's acceptance. I lived exactly the way I wanted to live, and yet, I still called myself a Christian (as many do). I felt empty and wondered if there was something more.

In the midst of that lifestyle, the mercy of God reached down, delivered me, and healed me. He only needed my "all-in," that moment when you finally surrender and make Jesus the Lord of your life. The gospel has the power to transform EVERYTHING when it is embraced fully. I am living proof. Only five years ago, I made the shift. I entered this totally new world full of limitless possibilities! And now, you are holding my story of redemption and the goodness and faithfulness of God!

My prayer for you in your journey ahead is that you would experience God's glory and the fear of the Lord with awe of His holiness, His power, and His presence in wonder and adoration for Him. You are created for such a time as this![2] You are created to walk in glorious freedom!

God is good!

Blessings,
Bryan Elliott

---

1. Brian Johnson, "To Our God," recorded October 2012, on *For the Sake of the World*, Bethel Music.
2. Esther 4:14

Spiritual Maturity

ASSESSMENT

Before you start the journey ahead, I encourage you to consider where you are in your walk with God. The hope we find in Jesus is a hope that transforms us into the image of Christ, reflecting His love in our motives, actions, and heart for others and ourselves. This is the process of sanctification and growing in spiritual maturity.

Personal reflection is an invitation to spend more time in the presence of God, meditating on His Word and His ways. I have found great reward in personal reflection when looking at my life and choices through a godly lens. I will often invite other mature believers into the process with me, asking for input in areas that need growth. Sometimes what God reveals requires repentance.

Set aside time to assess where you are in your journey with Christ using the following guide. Read through the list of words, asking God to help you see yourself clearly as you fill in the bubble you feel best represents your level of spiritual maturity. Remember, God does not expect our perfection; only He is perfect. He does, however, delight in our obedience to Him! God knows you and loves you as you are. He is excited to be on this journey with you and wants to see you grow.

SPIRITUAL MATURITY ASSESSMENT

	1	2	3	4	5	6	7	8	9	10	
Selfish Love (Worldly)	○	○	○	○	○	○	○	○	○	○	Sacrificial Love (Gospel)
Prideful	○	○	○	○	○	○	○	○	○	○	Humble
Tormented	○	○	○	○	○	○	○	○	○	○	Peaceful
Bitter	○	○	○	○	○	○	○	○	○	○	Merciful
Wounded	○	○	○	○	○	○	○	○	○	○	Healed
Religious (Law)	○	○	○	○	○	○	○	○	○	○	Relational (Grace)
Victim Mindset	○	○	○	○	○	○	○	○	○	○	Overcomer
Hopeless	○	○	○	○	○	○	○	○	○	○	Hope Filled
Depressed	○	○	○	○	○	○	○	○	○	○	Joy Filled
Fearful	○	○	○	○	○	○	○	○	○	○	Courageous
Condemned	○	○	○	○	○	○	○	○	○	○	Innocent
Self-Focus	○	○	○	○	○	○	○	○	○	○	Kingdom-Focus

SPIRITUAL MATURITY ASSESSMENT

Impulsive	1	2	3	4	5	6	7	8	9	10	Self-Controlled
Stingy	1	2	3	4	5	6	7	8	9	10	Generous
Prayerless	1	2	3	4	5	6	7	8	9	10	Prayerful
Easily Offended	1	2	3	4	5	6	7	8	9	10	Gracious
Impatient	1	2	3	4	5	6	7	8	9	10	Patient
Unforgiving	1	2	3	4	5	6	7	8	9	10	Forgiving
Control	1	2	3	4	5	6	7	8	9	10	Surrender
Unsatisfied	1	2	3	4	5	6	7	8	9	10	Content
Lukewarm	1	2	3	4	5	6	7	8	9	10	Passionate
Disconnected	1	2	3	4	5	6	7	8	9	10	Intimacy with God & People
Self-Reliant	1	2	3	4	5	6	7	8	9	10	God-Dependent
Know God Is Father	1	2	3	4	5	6	7	8	9	10	Know God As Father

After you have gone through the list, spend time in prayer, journaling and asking God to speak to you as you read the pages ahead. Ask Him to reveal Himself to you in new ways and refine the areas of your life that are contrary to His heart. Your journey ahead will be a great adventure. I know God will speak to you if you are willing to listen.

For a more extensive version of this assessment and additional resources, visit m46ministries.com/extras. Consider inviting others on the journey with you by reviewing the assessment results together. Trusted believers can help us spot blind spots and discover new areas of growth. God did not design us to walk this life alone, but in a community of believers who will encourage us and point us to Jesus daily.

*They are **more** precious **than gold**,*
...than much pure gold;
they are sweeter than honey,
...than honey from the honeycomb.

—Psalm 19:10, NIV

The rarest treasures of life are found in His truth.
That's why God's Word is prized like others prize the finest gold.
Sweeter also than honey are His living words—sweet words dripping
from the honeycomb!

—Psalm 19:10, TPT

Part One

Believing

"Christianity is about loving Jesus." — Bryn S. Elliott (my daughter, proud dad)

If you knew my daughter's story, you would come face to face with the redemptive power of Jesus. Bryn's life was unimaginably difficult. She was abused in secret from early childhood on for almost a decade, experienced multiple parental divorces, years of addiction and rehab, rapes, mental torment to the point of thinking she was insane, physical deterioration, loss of health, made countless bad choices, and lost her sister to murder when she was just 19. For years she woke up screaming that she wanted to die.

Now, at age 22, Bryn radiates the peace, love, and joy of the Lord. She is filled with the Word of God; the love of Jesus pours through her. She is an example of the radical transformation that happens when you give your life to Jesus. (Bryn's book, *Dying to Live*, shares her amazing testimony of God's goodness with the world.)

Like Bryn, God will redeem your story and use everything for your good, propelling you into your purpose and destiny. God has done it throughout the ages, and He's done it for my daughter and for me. He will do it for you, too, because He is the same yesterday, today, and forever! Just as He knew Bryn, God knew you before the creation of time! He knit you together in your mother's womb. God loves you and has an incredible plan for your life. More importantly, God wants a relationship with you! He sent His Son as our Saviour to die on your behalf so you could be included in His family. Faith comes by hearing and encountering the outrageously generous gospel of grace. It is a free gift available to everyone.

Before accepting Jesus, every person on earth longs to find purpose and feel complete. We have a God-sized hole that only He can fill through His Son, Jesus. Only Jesus can meet the deepest longing of your heart. God freely gave everything (His Son) as proof of His incredible love for us. Through His sacrifice, we get to step into our purpose: to know, love, and glorify God as He intended from the beginning. We deserved nothing, yet He gave us everything. And He offers this perfect redeeming love to everyone. Jesus' teachings, life, death, and resurrection are a testament to God's character and the length to which He will (and does) go for His children.

Choosing to believe in Jesus and accept His love gives us the ability to love as He does. 1 John 4:19 reads, "We love because He first loved us." Everything flows from simply loving Jesus and abiding in His presence. As Christians, in union with Jesus and filled with the Holy Spirit, we have the enormous honour of being the hands, feet, and voice of Jesus, growing in holiness as we become more like Him. We are being radically transformed every day. The gospel dramatically transformed my life, and He wants to transform yours, too! God is good! My life is a testimony of His goodness and how He makes all things work together for our good. I invite you to join me as I continue to explore the goodness of God in the land of the living!

For Further Reading: Psalm 139:13 and Hebrews 13:8

WHY JESUS?

Jesus answered, "I am the way and the truth and the life. No one comes to the Father except through Me."

—John 14:6

Regardless of what the world says, there is only one road to salvation, and His name is Jesus. "Why is Jesus the only way?" is an excellent question with several clear answers throughout God's Word and Jesus' life and teachings. Jesus was only 33 years old when He was crucified, resurrected, and ascended to heaven. He didn't start His ministry until He was 30. In just three years, Jesus set into motion a faith that spread across the world. Despite intense persecution against Christianity, more than 2.5 billion believers in Christ are alive today.[1] Why is this the case? Jesus.

In the words of C.S. Lewis, "Christianity, if false, is of no importance, and if true, of infinite importance. The only thing it cannot be is moderately important." [2] Jesus is not just another man. He is the Son of God. His life, ministry, and resurrection provide ample evidence of His deity. Through His resurrection, Jesus literally *conquered death* because He was sinless. (No other religious leader has predicted his death or resurrection, much less fulfilled that prophecy!)

The resurrection is the foundation for the good news. Without it, there is no hope for humanity as there would be no cure for sin. Because Christ conquered sin and death, those who submit to His Lordship have been given eternal life and are granted the right to be His co-heirs. Jesus came to show us the Father. He came to bring an entirely new covenant and reveal the true nature of God to the world, to see Him rightly. Jesus is the perfect image of the Father, who unconditionally loves every person on earth, and passionately desires to restore relationship with His created family. His life is a testimony of love, humility, mercy, compassion, and grace. He perfectly fulfills scriptural prophecies referring to the Messiah. Salvation comes through faith in Jesus alone, and those who know Him know what it means to be saved. No other religion has a sinless saviour who sacrificed everything to redeem those he loved. Jesus came as a man to show what is possible when we surrender and partner with God.

> And by the blood of His cross, everything in heaven and earth is brought back to Himself—back to its original intent, restored to innocence again!
>
> —Colossians 1:20, TPT

People who know me have witnessed the deep change within my heart over the past few years as my faith and relationship with Jesus has become more intimate. I know that my Redeemer lives, and through Him, I have life! Beyond a shadow of a doubt, I am confident that Jesus is the only way to salvation and the Father.

Invitation to Journey Deeper:

- What ways does the world say lead to truth? What happens when we try to find life in things of the world?
- What do you know about the love of Jesus? Why is He the only way?

For Further Reading: 1 Corinthians 15:17 and 2 Timothy 1:10

---

1. Aaron Earls, "7 Surprising Trends in Global Christianity in 2019," *Lifeway Research*, accessed February 18, 2022, https://research.lifeway.com/2019/06/11/7-surprising-trends-in-global-christianity-in-2019/.
2. Harry Farley, "10 times C.S. Lewis made the case for Christ," *Christianity Today*, accessed November 23, 2021, https://www.christiantoday.com/article/10.times.c.s.lewis.made.the.case.for.christ/96030.htm.

THE GOOD NEWS GOSPEL

For God so loved the world that He gave His one and only Son, that whoever believes in Him shall not perish but have eternal life. For God did not send His Son into the world to condemn the world, but to save the world through Him.

—John 3:16-17

The good news gospel is the story of creation, the fall of man, and man's redemption through the sacrificial death and resurrection of God's one and only Son, Jesus, as told in the Bible.

God is perfect in nature. He sets the standard, and His standard is perfect holiness. In our sinful state, His standard is unattainable. Think about it, how can any darkness be mixed with perfect, glorious light? They cannot exist together, which is exactly our problem. Sin separates us from God. Jesus tells us there is no one good, not even one. When sin separated humanity from God through Adam and Eve's rebellion, He set a plan in motion to restore what they lost in the fall. It was a plan that necessitated sacrifice, the forgiveness of sin, and the restoration of innocence.

God's love is relentless. His goodness is limitless. His faithfulness is unquestionable. His peace goes far beyond circumstance. His justice is perfect. It is not subjective. It is righteous. He is merciful. So, while we deserve eternal punishment, God provided His Son as a way back to our original place as righteous sons and daughters made Holy through Jesus' sacrifice. While we were still sinners, Christ died for us. He took our punishment.

Jesus is the only sinless person to have ever lived, making Him the perfect sacrifice. Jesus is THE WAY, the truth, and the life. There is no other saviour. There is no other messiah. There is no other adequate sacrifice other than God's one and only Son. No one comes to the

Father except through Him. Jesus made the way for us to return to the Father, and we get to decide where we will spend eternity based on our choices concerning Him.

Salvation has nothing to do with your ability and everything to do with His ability and His righteousness. It's received by faith in Jesus. Everyone who calls on the name of the Lord will be saved and experience eternal life. (Romans 10:13)

What does it cost? It will cost you everything. It cost Jesus His life! It will cost you yours too, but in a different way. Salvation requires you to make Jesus the Lord of your life. It requires a divine exchange, your life for His, your pain for His healing, your ashes for His beauty, your control for His Lordship, your plans for His *better way*.

God loves you. You are His workmanship. You are needed, special and unique by design. He has a beautiful plan and purpose for your life. He wants to meet you exactly where you are, *here and now,* regardless of your past or present situation. Jesus is in the business of making all things new! This is the good news gospel!

Invitation to Journey Deeper:

- When has someone sacrificed something for you? What was their motivation?
- How does it feel to know that God sacrificed Himself so that He could have a relationship with you?

For Further Reading: John 1:14; 19:1, Matthew 1:18; 26:67, Hebrews 2:9, Romans 5:8 and Luke 22:44

THE FALL OF MANKIND

For God so loved the world that He gave His one and only Son, that whoever believes in Him shall not perish but have eternal life.

—John 3:16

In the beginning, when God made the earth and everything in it, He created a garden filled with trees of all kinds called Eden. Eden was the idyllic home for Adam and Eve, the first man and first woman. God placed two specific trees in the middle of Eden: the Tree of Life and the Tree of Knowledge of Good and Evil. God specified that the first tree's fruit was good to eat, but the other should be left alone.

The fallen archangel, Satan, convinced Eve to eat fruit from the Tree of Knowledge of Good and Evil and told her she would not die as God said. Instead, he tells her in Genesis 3:4, "...God knows that when you eat from it your eyes will be opened, and you will be like God, knowing good and evil." Eve shared the fruit with Adam, and their eyes were immediately opened. As a result, sin entered the world in the forms of pride, deceit, and rebellion.

The word "sin" comes from the Greek word *hamartia,* meaning "a tragic flaw" or "to miss the mark." The "mark" in this context is God's perfect holiness and righteousness reflected in the person of Jesus Christ. Sin separates us from God. The original sin in the garden is the root of all evil, sickness, and death (both spiritual and physical). To sin means to live in opposition to God's original design. It means to live a lie or in a distorted, darkened understanding of our true identity. Darkness is the absence of light. Similarly, a lie is an absence of truth. When we receive the truth of who we are in Christ and the truth of our loving heavenly Father, the light switches on. The lie no longer exists, like the darkness.

It is important to understand that Adam and Eve experienced God in perfect relationship before the fall—safe, secure, filled with love, peace, and joy. They saw God rightly. God designed us in His image with free will for His glory and the joy of relationship. When sin entered the world through Adam and Eve's wilful act of rebellion, God had His redemption plan in place already.

For thousands of years, God's people continued to rebel against Him. Regardless of how far His people strayed, God promised to send a Saviour that would redeem their brokenness once and for all. Because He is a perfect, faithful Father, God sent His Son, Jesus, to bear our punishment and destroy the work of sin and evil once and for all! Jesus, the only one without sin, became the ultimate sacrifice so that we could live in union with the Father once again.

God's love never changes. He could never love you more. He could never love you less. God sees you through the finished work of Jesus on the cross—when you receive Him, you become one with Him. No matter your sin, no matter how far you have fallen, He wants to restore you. He wants a relationship with you!

Invitation to Journey Deeper:

- What are the characteristics of a "perfect" relationship?
- How did pride play a part in the fall of mankind?
- Why does God work so hard to reconcile His children back to Him?

For Further Reading: Genesis 1-3

CREATED WITH
PURPOSE

Before the fall of man, Adam and Eve enjoyed a perfect relationship with God. As His children, they saw Him correctly. However, after they rebelled against God and the power of sin was unleashed onto the earth, their lens was skewed and their relationship torn apart. Instead of viewing God as a loving Father, man began to view God as a distant punisher to rebel against (Satan's perspective). They no longer lived as God's children but as orphans.

God is a perfect Father. There is no evil in Him! He loves His children more than any earthly parent ever could. When we walk away from Him, it grieves Him. When we choose the enemy, His heart breaks. Satan seeks to kill, steal, and destroy our hope, freedom, joy, and relationships. Like Adam and Eve, the enemy wants us to feel naked and alone. He wants us to hide our shame in the dark... to be fatherless.

Thankfully, Jesus came to restore the relationship Adam and Even first enjoyed with God in the garden. In Christ, there is no more shame or punishment. Sin is defeated! We are fully accepted sons and daughters, safe and secure, fully known, and unconditionally loved by our gracious Father.

Slow down for a moment and take this in:

You are the pinnacle of God's creation. You are His crowning jewel. He knew you before He created the world. You are His design. You are the object of His love. You are fully known and fully loved. God wants a personal relationship with you more than you could imagine. You are a son or daughter of God. You are His family.

He made you in His image! God made us to be like Jesus. Jesus said we would do even greater things than Him as we are seated with Him in heavenly places and have been given the Holy Spirit. He created you with a destiny that requires Him and His body (the Church) to accomplish together. He loves you. He values you. There is no striving or pressure in Him. Simple obedience is true success. He wants you to succeed. He is for you. As you mature in Him, growing in awareness of your completeness in Him, your destiny unfolds. You inherit all that Jesus is and all that He has. He came to give abundant life. Jesus is abundant life! Eternal life! He gave Himself to us.

This is the mind-boggling gospel. This is the truth that sets us free! While we cannot fully understand it, we can fully receive and experience it as we walk with God and learn to love like Him.

SON OF MAN

For He knew all about us before we were born and He destined us from the beginning to share the likeness of His Son. This means the Son is the oldest among a vast family of brothers and sisters who will become just like Him.

—Romans 8:29, TPT

Jesus gets us. He is fully man and fully God. Born into the world in a first-century version of a barn to parents who were by all means average, Jesus lived, learned, worked, suffered, and existed on this physical earth.

Yet, Jesus lived the human experience *without sin.* He experienced the pain, rejection, betrayal, and temptation we all face. But because Jesus is also fully God, He was and is completely sovereign, perfect, and holy.

He is the divine portrait, the true likeness of the invisible God, and the firstborn heir of all creation. For in Him was created the universe of things, both in the heavenly realm and on the earth, all that is seen and all that is unseen. Every seat of power, realm of government, principality, and authority—it all exists through Him and for His purpose!

—Colossians 1:15-16, TPT

Jesus is the "firstborn" of all creation. All creation originates in Him and through Him. When sin entered the picture in Genesis 3, His relationship with creation was broken, and subsequently, all relationships became compromised. However, through Jesus' death and resurrection, He reconciled creation to Himself once more. We can stand firm in the truth of Jesus' words in John 11:25-26, "...I am the resurrection and the life. The one who believes in Me will live, even though they die; and whoever lives by believing in Me will never die. Do you believe this?"

He adopts anyone who submits to His Lordship into His family and conforms them into His image. The deeper their relationship with Jesus grows, the more like Him they will become. And because He is love, those who follow Him will eventually look like love too, through the power of the Holy Spirit.

Regardless of my countless mistakes and shortcomings, I know that Jesus loves and accepts me with the tender love of a perfect father. Because I am fully known, accepted, loved, and forgiven, I am free to be myself without the need to hide. I know He understands what I am going through and makes me more like Him every day. It is a journey, and He is the destination.

Invitation to Journey Deeper:

- How does it feel to know that Jesus experienced life on earth just like you and me?
- How would you describe the perfect love of a father?
- What gets in the way of you living and loving like Jesus (i.e., representing Jesus on earth)?

For Further Reading: Matthew 16:27; 24:30 and John 16:7

POWER

IN HIS NAME

To discover who Jesus is, one must only look to His name. Jesus, the Greek translation of the Hebrew name Yeshua, means "Saviour." Christ is Greek for "*Messiah*" (*mashiach* in Hebrew), Jesus' official title in Hebrew. Jesus Christ, *Yeshua Hamashiach*, Jesus the Messiah, is our Saviour and Messiah. He came to set us free from the law of sin and save us from death. Jesus is who His name says He is. That's why there is power in the name of Jesus! Consider some of Jesus' many names as listed in Scripture:

- Jesus is God *(2 Peter 1:1)*
- Our Advocate *(1 John 2:1)*
- Lamb of God *(John 1:29)*
- The Resurrection and The Life *(John 11:25)*
- Lord of lords *(1 Timothy 6:15)*
- Man of Sorrows *(Isaiah 53:3)*
- Head of the Church *(Colossians 1:18)*
- Master *(Matthew 8:19)*
- Faithful and True Witness *(Revelation 3:14)*
- Rock *(1 Corinthians 10:4)*
- High Priest *(Hebrews 6:20)*
- The Door *(John 10:9)*
- Living Water *(John 4:10)*
- Bread of Life *(John 6:35)*
- Rose of Sharon *(Song of Solomon 2:1)*
- Alpha and Omega *(Revelation 22:13)*
- True Vine *(John 15:1)*

- Messiah *(Luke 2:11)*
- Teacher *(John 3:2)*
- Holy One of God *(Mark 1:24)*
- Mediator *(1 Timothy 2:5)*
- Beloved *(Ephesians 1:6)*
- Vine *(John 15:5)*
- Carpenter *(Mark 6:3)*
- Good Shepherd *(John 10:11)*
- Light of the World *(John 8:12)*
- Image of the Invisible God *(Colossians 1:15)*
- The Word *(John 1:1)*
- Chief Cornerstone *(Ephesians 2:20)*
- Saviour *(John 4:42)*
- Servant *(Matthew 12:18)*
- Pioneer and Perfecter of Our Faith *(Hebrews 12:2)*
- The Almighty *(Revelation 1:8)*
- Everlasting Father *(Isaiah 9:6)*
- Lion of the Tribe of Judah *(Revelation 5:5)*
- I AM *(John 8:58)*
- King of kings *(1 Timothy 6:15)*
- Prince of Peace *(Isaiah 9:6)*
- Bridegroom *(Matthew 9:15)*
- Only Begotten Son *(John 3:16)*
- Wonderful Counsellor *(Isaiah 9:6)*
- Immanuel *(Matthew 1:23)*
- Son of Man *(Matthew 20:28)*
- The Amen and The Ruler Over God's Creation *(Revelation 3:14)*
- King of the Jews *(Mark 15:26)*
- Prophet *(Matthew 21:11)*
- Redeemer *(Job 19:25)*
- Anchor *(Hebrews 6:19)*
- Bright Morning Star *(Revelation 22:16)*
- The Way, The Truth, and The Life *(John 14:6)*
- A Life Giving Spirit *(1 Corinthians 15:45)*

DOUBT AND PRIDE

For the wages of sin is death, but the gift of God is eternal life in Christ Jesus our Lord.

—Romans 6:23

Pride is often easy to see in others but is very difficult to see in ourselves. It is a state of deception (which is why it is not always obvious). Even when our pride is exposed, we often justify and rationalise it. According to C.S. Lewis, "Pride leads to every other vice: it is the complete anti-God state of mind... it is pride which has been the chief cause of misery in every nation and every family since the world began."[1]

Strangely enough, pride often seeps in through Satan's primary weapon: doubt. Doubt attempts to erode our trust, which leads to unbelief. That unbelief creates independence from God, which is a form of pride. This was the original temptation, to doubt God in the garden, and the result was pride and the fall of man.

We all experience different forms of doubt from time to time, but it wasn't doubt that caused the fall. It was Adam and Eve's response to doubt that resulted in separation from God. The same is true for us.

Unlike us, Jesus meets God's perfect standard. He paid our debt so we can enter the presence of a Holy God. We have a chance to accept this gift only while we are alive on earth (and we all know how fleeting that is). The other option is an eternity in hell, separated from God and His goodness, grace, and mercy. There is no in-between.

Jesus came as a perfect sacrifice for our sins through grace by faith alone. We deserved hell, but Jesus took the penalty for our sin upon Himself. His blood paid the full price of our redemption. No shame—ever. No condemnation—ever. We are now in Him! From this point, we are holy, and step-by-step, we are renewing our minds to this truth. The truth sets us free!

In a 2019 interview, Jordan Peterson, a clinical psychologist, indicated that people have a great capacity for evil and that it is dangerous to think we are good. Instead, he says we do things that "approximate good."[2]

No doubt, there is potential for good in human nature, but we are all greatly flawed. Even a good person is only good *most* of the time. Every one of us is sinful some of the time. 2 Corinthians 10:12 says, "We do not dare to classify or compare ourselves with some who commend themselves. When they measure themselves by themselves and compare themselves with themselves, they are not wise."

The standard of perfection is our problem. It cannot be earned or measured by human standards. Romans 6:23 says, "...the wages of sin is death..." No matter how big or small, any sin qualifies us for death. Therefore, we are all equally guilty and owe a debt that is impossible to pay on our own. This is a terrifying concept and leads to my immense gratefulness that Jesus paid my debt in full!

Before I made Jesus Lord of my life, I seemed good by the world's standards. I was nice, generous, honest, fit, and wealthy. But, I had no idea of the true condition of my heart. After I made Jesus Lord, the process of transformation began. I am a different person filled with His peace, compassion, and love more than I could have ever imagined. The Lord is my best friend, my Father. I spend time with Him, no longer out of a sense of religious obligation but out of love and genuine enjoyment.

Just think, while we were wicked and rebellious, Jesus loved us so much that He died for us! We become one with Jesus in His death and permanently unite with Him in resurrection life. We get to see God rightly and experience Him once again! Freedom!

Invitation to Journey Deeper:

- How has pride kept you from knowing and experiencing the fullness of God?
- What does the world say is good? What is *actually* good according to Scripture?
- How does it feel to know that Jesus died for your freedom? How does knowing that change your way forward?

For Further Reading: Matthew 27

---

1. Thomas A. Tarrants, "Pride and Humility," *C.S. Lewis Institute*, accessed November 23, 2021, https://www.cslewisinstitute.org/Pride_and_Humility_SinglePage.
2. Jordan Peterson, "The Universal Ethic of Approximating Reciprocity," *YouTube*, accessed November 23, 2021, https://www.youtube.com/watch?v=xahmyVtzuNE.

A SIMPLE CHOICE

If my people, who are called by My name, will humble themselves and pray and seek My face and turn from their wicked ways, then I will hear from heaven, and I will forgive their sin and will heal their land.

—2 Chronicles 7:14

Our free choice and response to God determine our eternal outcome. *It's that simple.* We have the decision to receive the loving, healing power of Jesus... or not. It's our choice to return to Him and receive the embrace, the ring, and the robe like the prodigal son in Jesus' parable... or not. In the end, there are only two options: a reunion with God or separation from God, where no good exists. The choice is ours. God has given us free will and the ability to make choices with consequences, good or bad.

As C.S. Lewis said, "There are two kinds of people in this world. Those who bend their knee to God and say to Him, 'Your will be done,' or those who refuse to bend their knee to God and God says to them, 'Your will be done.'"[1] He also went on to say, "...the damned are in one sense successful, rebels to the end; that the doors of hell are locked on the inside... just as the blessed, forever submitting to obedience, become through all eternity more and more free."[2]

Because God is holy and cannot go against His own nature, He is committed to righteousness. In fact, He loves righteousness more than His own creation and will protect it at all costs (go back and read the story of Noah's Ark if you aren't convinced). God is a fiery, *holy* God who cast Satan out of heaven in an instant like a lightning bolt, never to return because of his unrighteousness. As such, the cross is about righteousness as much as it is about love. Jesus submitted to being crucified because He loves us and so we could receive His righteousness.

According to Brian Simmons, author of *The Passion Translation*:

In essence, "sin . . . righteousness . . . and judgment are related to three persons." Sin is related to Adam, for it was through Adam that sin entered humanity (Romans 5:12). Righteousness is related to Christ, because it comes through Him, and He has become our righteousness (1 Corinthians 1:30). Judgment is related to Satan, for the pure works of Christ bring judgment to the works of Satan. If we do not embrace Christ's righteousness, we will share Satan's judgment.[3]

God is a God of perfect justice, and justice means you get fair treatment (or you get what you deserve). The suffering of Jesus, one without sin, demonstrates the seriousness of God's judgement. Jesus did not come to abolish the Law but to fulfil it, and when we accept Jesus, He becomes our righteousness.[4] We are either in or out, saved by grace with eternal life or condemned to hell for our sin. The choice is ours.

Jesus took the death penalty for our sins. To come under the judgement of the Living God is the most terrifying thing of all! But by His mercy and grace, we have the opportunity to choose Him and receive what we don't deserve: eternity with God. We never know when our time will come to an end on the earth or when Jesus will return. Our eternity all comes down to a decision. Not making a decision is still a decision. We get to choose heaven or hell by conscious decision or no-decision. It is a revelation of His love, kindness, and compassion that leads our hearts to repentance. My prayer is that all will choose Jesus.

Invitation to Journey Deeper:

- Have you submitted yourself to God, or are you living in rebellion?
- How does submission lead to freedom?
- What areas of your life are difficult to surrender? Why?

For Further Reading: Luke 15:11-32, Hebrews 10:31 and Genesis 6-9

1. "Book Review: The Great Divorce," *Presbyformed*, accessed November 23, 2021, https://presbyformed.com/2016/10/05/book-review-the-great-divorce-by-c-s-lewis/.

2. C.S. Lewis, *The Problem of Pain, in The Complete C. S. Lewis Signature Classics* (San Francisco: Harper San Francisco, 2002), 419–20.

3. "John 16:11, *The Passion Translation*," https://www.bible.com/bible/1849/JHN.16.TPT, Biblegateway.com, accessed November 23, 2021, https://www.biblegateway.com/passage/?search=john+16%3A11&version=TPT#en-TPT-8087.

4. "The Law" refers to commands given to the Israelites in the Old Testament in order to uphold their covenant with God. Hebrews 10 describes the New Covenant in Christ based not on merit, but the freedom offered through God's grace and forgiveness. For more, see "The Old Covenant vs. The New Covenant" on page 68.

KEY POINTS

TO THE GOSPEL

- God loved us before we were formed in our mother's womb and intended for us to be His partners in bringing heaven to earth. *(Psalm 139:13-14, Ephesians 1:4)*

- When man rebelled, there was a permanent separation from God, and man was subject to His judgement for sin and the introduction of death. Our human nature is sinful, and the wages of sin is death — physical, spiritual, and eternal. *(Romans 6:23)*

- God's justice demands death for sin. *(John 8:24)*

- Those who don't think about their accountability to God or do not believe in the spiritual realities are spiritually dead and deceived. *(Ephesians 2:1)*

- Jesus came to restore the relationship between God and man and defeat death. He fully knows you, loves you, values you, and has a great plan for your life. His kindness leads us to repentance. He is rich in mercy and compassion. *(2 Timothy 1:10, Ephesians 2:4, Jeremiah 29:11, Romans 2:4)*

- Satan comes only to steal, kill, and destroy. Jesus came that we may have life and have it to the full. *(John 10:10)*

- Jesus reveals the character and nature of God. In the words of Jesus, "Anyone who has seen Me, has seen the Father" *(John 14:9).*

- After Jesus died and rose again, defeating death and reconciling God and man, the Holy Spirit came to establish God's kingdom on earth, reclaim the nations, and glorify Jesus. *(John 16:7-14)*

- Salvation requires one to recognise their need to be reconciled and receive forgiveness from Jesus. *(1 John 1:9)*

- Everyone who calls on the name of the Lord will be saved. This is God's will. *(Romans 10:13, 1 Timothy 2:3-4)*

- Since we are His true children, we qualify to share His treasures, for indeed, we are heirs of God. Joined with Christ, we also inherit all that He is and all that He has. *(Romans 8:17; 1 Peter 3:9)*

SALVATION IS OURS

If you declare with your mouth, "Jesus is Lord," and believe in your
heart that God raised Him from the dead, you will be saved.

—Romans 10:9

At its core, the gospel is about how much God loves people and much
less about how lost they are, although the Bible is clear about the cost of
sin (the things we do against God's commands that separate us from
Him). Think about how short life is in the context of eternity. If the
gospel is true, then it's the most important truth we could ever know.
We should approach our salvation with fear and trembling.

If you are not sure if you are saved, you can give your life to Jesus right
now, wherever you are, whatever condition your life is in. God sees
your heart and wants a relationship with you! His forgiveness is for all.
His grace is limitless!

I was 13 when I first gave my heart to the Lord. It was a simple
moment. I had a strong feeling to tell my parents my decision to
become a Christian, and so I did. Not long after, I was baptised at our
Baptist church... and that was about it. There was no dramatic change
in my heart or spirit. Life went on as usual. For a while, at least.

Later that year, my brother accidentally shot himself, and my parents'
marriage fell apart in the aftermath. My small flame of faith slowly
burnt out, though I would continue to call myself a Christian.

More than 30 years later, *everything* changed in November 2015 when
my daughter Bryn and I visited a prayer group in New Brunswick. It
was there that a community of mature and passionate believers
welcomed me in and began to mentor me. A deep hunger to read the
Bible filled me, and gradually, my relationship with Jesus was rekin-
dled. This was the first time that I truly made Jesus the Lord of my life

and made my faith my own, not based on the beliefs of my family or anyone else.

In November 2019, Bryn and I again visited the prayer group. This was during Bryn's most intense transition period that began a month prior to a deliverance session. During this stay, I attended an in-depth teaching on grace over a three-day period with Dean Briggs, an intercessory missionary, author, and speaker.

As the flame within me grew stronger, and with a new understanding of baptism, I decided to be baptised again alongside Bryn, who had decided to give her life to the Lord. Going under the water, my old self died with Christ on the cross. I came back up as a new man and a new creation, alive in Christ. I look back on that fall day as one of the sweetest moments of my life. Although there were no fireworks or obvious power encounters, Bryn and I were on a totally new life trajectory.

"The Kingdom of God is for the brokenhearted."

—Fred Rogers[1]

The broken hearted are the people aware that they are spiritually bankrupt and helpless, humble and remorseful over their sins. These are the ones who will inherit the Kingdom of God. They know they need a saviour and are ready to receive the gift of salvation expressed through the gospel.

If we truly believe that we are sinners in need of a saviour and that Jesus Christ is our risen Saviour, all we have to do is simply declare it out loud and receive His salvation by faith. This is the gift of grace through faith.

Invitation to Journey Deeper:

- Do you believe that Jesus Christ is the risen Saviour? Why or why not?
- Read Matthew 5:3-12. How does your heart reflect the eight qualities outlined in Jesus' *Sermon on the Mount*?
- If you want to make Jesus the Lord of your life, see "A Prayer for the New Believer" on page 44 and "Next Steps for the New Believer" on page 45.

For Further Reading: Romans 10:9 and Matthew 5:3-12

---

1. Geoffrey James, "45 Quotes from Mr. Rogers We All Need Today," *INC*, accessed November 23, 2021, https://www.inc.com/geoffrey-james/45-quotes-from-mr-rogers-that-we-all-need-today.html.

A PRAYER FOR THE
NEW BELIEVER

If you are ready to surrender your heart and make Jesus the Lord of your life, I invite you to pray the following prayer:

Lord Jesus,

Thank You for loving me. I admit that I am a sinner, and I believe You died for my sins. I repent and ask for Your forgiveness. I believe You are the Son of God, that You died and rose again. I renounce Satan. I receive You now as my personal Lord and Saviour. I invite You into my heart and to manage my life from this day forward. I surrender my entire life to You. I choose to serve You with all of my heart, soul, mind, and body. I receive Your glorious gift of grace, love, and eternal life! Thank You for adopting me as Your own. I am a child of God! I am born again! I dedicate my life to You and declare Jesus, You are Lord. Amen!

If you prayed that prayer from your heart, you have been born again! You are a child of God, starting with a clean slate. You have entered into a personal relationship with Jesus Christ! Your identity is no longer that of a sinner. You are saved by grace. Sin is defeated! You are a saint, and His righteousness is yours now and forever. You are holy. Your old nature is dead, and the process of renewing your mind has begun. You are one with Him!

NEXT STEPS FOR THE
NEW BELIEVER

Choosing to make Jesus Lord of your life is a decision worth celebrating! Mark today's date and write it down in your Bible or somewhere special. This is the day of new beginnings! As you enter into relationship with Him, I encourage you to take the following steps to anchor and grow your faith.

01

Read the Bible. It is vital that you get to know who God is, what He has done, and what He will do. Challenge yourself to read the Bible in a year (many guides are available to walk you through this process). The Gospels of Matthew, Mark, Luke, and John are a great place to start as you learn more about Jesus and His ministry on earth.

02

Make prayer a daily habit. Developing any relationship requires time and communication. Set aside time every day to pray and listen for God's voice. Consider journaling your prayers to help you focus your time with Him. Tell God what you're thankful for or what needs you have. He wants to hear it all!

03

Find a healthy, Bible-believing church. We need other believers around us to grow spiritually. Fellowship and communion through worship, prayer, and the study of God's Word with the body of Christ sharpen us and prepare us for the road ahead. Don't be afraid to check out a few churches, and make sure to connect with the one you choose!

04

Engage in a small group and find a mentor. We need others to disciple us in the ways of the kingdom—worldview, principles, and lifestyle. Get involved with a small group or Bible study to help guide and challenge you in your faith journey. Begin to pray and look for wise counsel who can mentor you one-on-one. Don't be afraid to ask!

05

Get baptised. Water baptism is an essential outward symbol that declares our faith in Christ to the world. What's more, it is a powerful physical reminder and spiritual activation of the fullness of the grace we have received through faith. It is a biblical practice that brings us into the deeper aspects of our union with Christ and greater maturity. This is not intended to be a religious act or performance.

06

Talk about it! Don't keep the good God has done in your life to yourself. Share your journey with family, friends, and whoever else God may put in your path. We are blessed to be a blessing, and God wants to use your story for His kingdom!

He knows we are His since He has also stamped His seal of love over our hearts and has given us the Holy Spirit like an engagement ring is given to a bride—a down payment of the blessings to come!

—2 Corinthians 1:22, TPT

CHOOSING TO FOLLOW HIM

Because His heart was focused on the joy of knowing that you would be His, He endured the agony of the cross and conquered its humiliation, and now sits exalted at the right hand of the throne of God!

—Hebrews 12:2b, TPT

When someone truly gives their heart to Jesus, everything changes from that point on. There is a heartfelt desire and commitment to leading a new life, living in God's ways. The process of becoming more like Jesus is not optional. The Bible says that faith is an actual "substance" and the evidence required to prove the unseen.

When I finally made Jesus Lord of my life, the Holy Spirit began to transform everything about me. Before then, I had not experienced the unshakable Kingdom of righteousness, peace, and joy in the Holy Spirit that I do now. I had no idea such peace was possible while on earth.

Salvation begins with a choice to believe and a heart of repentance that acknowledges our sinful nature. It comes from a desire to turn from sin and towards God in humility, choosing to love what God loves and hate what God hates. Repentance turns our hearts to God and aligns us with His truth, from our ways to God's ways.

Those of us who know Jesus are set free from the slavery of sin. However, that does not mean we are free from temptations the enemy puts in our path. The Bible is clear that the enemy roams the earth looking for someone to devour like a lion. In these moments, we have the opportunity to turn our face to Jesus to receive His strength and grace. Difficult circumstances help us face our weaknesses and teach us to increasingly rely on the Lord.

Salvation is much more than just a prayer. It marks the day you become a disciple of Jesus. As you grow in awareness of your identity in Christ, you will awaken more and more to God's original design for you. In other words, you will still sin, but you will sin less and less as your mind, emotions, and spirit are made more like Christ through abiding in Him. From the moment you choose to believe and turn to Jesus, He gives you the faith needed to walk in His footsteps.

> *Now faith is confidence in what we hope for and assurance about what we do not see.*
>
> —*Hebrews 11:1*

Invitation to Journey Deeper:

- Have you made Jesus the absolute Lord of your life? If not, what's stopping you?
- If you already know Jesus as your Lord and Saviour, what do you remember about the day you invited Him into your life? What has changed since then?
- Pause and check in with the Holy Spirit. How is He calling you to grow in faith and maturity?

For Further Reading: Hebrews 11:1, Romans 6:6 7 and 1 Peter 5:8

BAPTISM IN WATER

Now, if anyone is enfolded into Christ, he has become an entirely new person. All that is related to the old order has vanished. Behold, everything is fresh and new. And God has made all things new, and reconciled us to Himself, and given us the ministry of reconciling others to God.

—2 Corinthians 5:17-18, TPT

Water baptism is a powerful physical sign of Christ's transformative power. The Bible is very clear that water baptism is necessary. John the Baptist baptised Jesus. It marks someone as a Christian and a member of the family of God. Just as we celebrate the resurrection of Christ from the grave on Easter, coming out of the baptism water is a celebration of the new life of a believer.

When I was baptised at 13 in my family's Baptist church, I didn't have a true understanding of the power of baptism. I thought it was simply a public expression of my faith as part of my salvation experience. This is undoubtedly true, but not at all complete. Baptism is much more than a public expression.

Salvation comes from faith through grace. The biblical practice of baptism, as modeled in Acts 8:26-40, is necessary to mature us in our faith and in the process of sanctification. When I truly understood the significance of water baptism, I enthusiastically chose to be baptised again as an adult alongside my daughter, Bryn, on November 27, 2019. This moment was not about seeking an emotional experience or engaging in a religious act. Rather, it was an exclamation mark on my faith, being co-crucified and co-resurrected with Christ. It was my moment to lay down my life once and for all for the freedom Christ died to give me.

The Passion Translation refers to the Holy Spirit as "the Spirit of Grace" in Hebrews 10:29. The Holy Spirit is the dispenser and Lord of grace. To be filled with the Holy Spirit means that He fills you with the grace (spiritual power) to live pure, holy, and undefiled.

Baptism gives us every reason to rejoice. It symbolises the new life we receive when we submit to the lordship of Jesus. It signals that we are purified from the effects of sin, reborn in Christ, and are now His co-heirs.

Water baptism brings us into the deeper realms of Christ through symbolic co-crucifixion. Under the water, our sins are symbolically "buried and the power of sin is broken. Fully identified with Christ, they are buried with Him and [we] are raised to a new life in the power and resurrection of Jesus."[1]

When we receive Jesus as our Lord and Saviour and submit to His transformative power, our spirit becomes a new creation that is one with Christ. The act of baptism allows us to literally die to our old self and be raised to new life in Jesus and filled with the Holy Spirit. Jesus' death destroyed the grip of Satan.

The old self is now dead.

Believe it!

Sin has no dominion over you.

That being the case, we must surrender our lives, hopes, and dreams to Jesus. In Christ, there is no condemnation. We fully join Him in His death and are now one with Him. As we come out of the water, we experience the fullness of how God created us to live. Our new self naturally follows God in righteousness and holiness.

Invitation to Journey Deeper:

- Have you been water baptised? If not, what is holding you back?
- Do you walk in the confidence of your new life as a believer? Why or why not?
- In what ways can you open your senses to experience the presence of Jesus and to hear His voice?

For Further Reading: 2 Corinthians 5:17 and John 3:5

---

1. "Baptism," *Fuller*, accessed December 30, 2021, https://www.fuller.edu/next-faithful-step/resources/baptism/.

AN ACT OF SURRENDER

Whoever wants to be My disciple must deny themselves and take up their cross and follow Me.

—Matthew 16:24

I once had a long talk with a young man in which I answered all of his questions and objections about Christianity. We discussed my story, Jesus, unconditional acceptance, grace, eternity, heaven, hell, the history of the church, science, etc. In the end, I asked him, "If Christianity were true, would you become a Christian?" His answer totally shocked me. He said no. He wanted to do life his own way, no matter the consequence. He was a bright, engaging man who represented a tragically large portion of the population.

Why might this be the case? Several reasons come to mind. The obvious answer is that the god of this age has blinded the eyes of unbelievers. People often hear a message of condemnation, hell, and descriptions of an angry, distant God rather than the true gospel of grace, the gospel that describes how much God loves us. To receive this love, however, entails complete surrender.

Surrendering means giving up oneself to become like Jesus. Anything that doesn't line up with His commands must go. I am a living testimony of what it looks like to give your life to Jesus and can affirm that this is the most freeing experience available to man.

Even things that appear good on the outside can be evil and lead to sin. No matter how much pleasure sin may afford in the moment, it always ends in death. In contrast, whatever you give up to follow Jesus now will reap immeasurable rewards forever, including eternal life. (This is counter-cultural to the postmodern focus on the self and individualism.)

Belief in Jesus is offensive to our flesh. The flesh refers to our sinful nature that will not submit to the will of God. Our flesh is at war with God. In order to love God, we must submit to Jesus, who gives us power over our flesh and a new mind and spirit that are one with Him.

Another reason many avoid the message of Christianity is that it hurts our pride to find out we aren't as good as we think we are and that our hard work will never be enough to make it to heaven. If we break any of God's commandments at any point in our life, we are guilty under the Law. It is never about what we can achieve; it's about what Christ has accomplished for us to simply receive.

If we committed a crime and went to court and told the judge that we are a good person and listed all the positive things we had done in our lives, it would not make us innocent of the crime we committed. How much greater is God's standard of perfection?

Christ becomes our perfection; His righteousness becomes our righteousness.

As I reflect on my time with this young man, the vast majority of our conversation focused on "facts" and far too little on the love of God and the power of the gospel to save. More importantly, I realize that for much of my life, I was just like him, though perhaps not as overtly. I was not willing to walk out what I believed.

There is a very big difference between belief and faith.

Belief comes from an understanding of truth and results in head knowledge. But faith is what gives us the confidence and trust to make Jesus the Lord of our lives.

Many "believers" do not have faith. We say we are Christians, but we are still the Lord of our own lives. Ultimately, it is our heart position and free will that God honours.

Invitation to Journey Deeper:

- What would it cost you to surrender your life to Jesus?
- What do you risk losing in order to gain what is worth more than gold?

For Further Reading: John 20:20 and James 1:2; 2:10

KNOWN BY THEIR FRUIT

A good tree cannot bear bad fruit, and a bad tree cannot bear good fruit. Every tree that does not bear good fruit is cut down and thrown into the fire. Thus, by their fruit you will recognize them. "Not everyone who says to Me, 'Lord, Lord,' will enter the Kingdom of heaven, but only the one who does the will of My Father who is in heaven."

—Matthew 7:18-21

Prior to 2016, I had no idea what being a true believer really meant. The gospel is the power of God to transform and cannot be watered down for our convenience. Accepting the gospel is about accepting the full life-changing invitation into the Kingdom of God. It is the small and narrow road that leads to life, and sadly, as Jesus says, very few find it. We are all in or all out.

It is our choice whether to remain the master of our own lives or give everything to Jesus. Scripture says that when we do, we will be known by the fruit of the Holy Spirit in our lives.

When your lives bear abundant fruit, you demonstrate that you are My mature disciples who glorify My Father!

—John 15:8, TPT

Giving your life to Jesus is not a casual decision or a partial commitment. When you surrender your life, it means you are no longer your own, and you now live for Him. Far too often, people think they can go back to their lives, feeling good about their supposed eternal salvation, and wind up changing very little about their everyday life. We can't say a quick prayer to avoid hell and still be lord of our own lives. That is not the gospel.

With that said, salvation is a free gift of faith. God looks into our hearts and wants us more than we can imagine. The Lord is incredibly gracious and understands our unique struggles and journey. He is faithful and never gives up on anyone on their path to salvation. Jesus came to seek and save all that was lost. God's will is that none shall perish.

And when we do choose Him, it changes things. It changes things immediately, and it changes things little by little the more we understand our Lord and His ways. With each decision to pursue Him, we become more like Him. We let go of our old ways and are transformed by the power of the Holy Spirit. We begin to bear good fruit. This fruit not only becomes a display of God's goodness on earth, but it also begins to bless others with its sweetness. After all, what good is fruit if not for sharing?

Invitation to Journey Deeper:

- Read Galatians 5:22-23. Which fruit do you see in your life? Which fruit do you desire?
- Where do you stand in your walk with the Lord? Are you all in or all out?
- What is God calling you to in this season? Pause to reflect and ask the Holy Spirit to give you clarity and discernment.

For Further Reading: Matthew 7:13-14

DISCIPLE-MAKERS:
THE (OFTEN) MISSING LINK IN THE CHURCH

*Then He said to them all: "Whoever wants to be My disciple must
deny themselves and take up their cross daily and follow Me."*

—Luke 9:23

Why don't people always experience transformation after making Jesus
Lord of their lives? Why do some people find themselves re-committing
their lives to Jesus after repeatedly going astray? The answer is because
they have not been discipled. They have not been parented in the faith,
and as a result, they remain "only converts." Salvation is the inception
point of entering the Kingdom and beginning our journey with God.

In the words of my daughter Bryn, "Salvation is a free gift of justifica-
tion, a personal revival. But, in order to grow mature believers, conver-
sion must be followed up with discipleship. A personal revival must be
followed by personal reformation. Walking in discipleship is the
process of sanctification."

Discipleship has nothing to do with religious activity or being a "good"
Christian. Rather, it is the biblical method of cultivating intimacy with
God while becoming like Jesus and leads to accelerated transformation.

Think of discipleship as a practice. A disciple is a *practicer*. A disciple
of Jesus is one who practices what He teaches. Every Christian is called
to be a disciple and disciple-maker, introducing people to Jesus and
teaching them to be like Him. Jesus, the ultimate disciple-maker, repro-
duced Himself in His disciples so they could disciple others to become
like Him. We are called to lead and be led just the same.

I tried life and "Christianity" my way for many years, and it did not
play out well. In 2016, when I truly made Jesus Lord of my life, my
priorities changed to follow suit through the process of discipleship. I

discovered the importance of spending time with God in prayer, connecting with believers, reading the Word, worshiping, journaling, and learning to hear the voice of God.

In time, I came to value the growth that came from seasons in the wilderness, learning to depend on God, engaging in healing and deliverance, surrendering daily, being mentored, and deepening my relationship with God. In short, abiding in Him and cultivating the manifest presence of Jesus.

All of these practices encompassed my discipling journey. By submitting to godly leadership and practicing spiritual disciplines, I built a deep foundation. Now, I can pass on what I've learnt through experience to others.

We learn to imitate Jesus and to steward His presence on earth as we are transformed into His image. Jesus' greatest commandment is to love. Love is the ultimate result of discipleship and is a sign of spiritual maturity. What's more, the Greatest Commandment (to love God and others) fuels the Great Commission. Transformed people transform people, families, systems, etc.—everywhere and everything they are called to!

We are called to develop relationships with people inside and outside of the church to demonstrate the love of Jesus and manifest the Kingdom of God to the world. The best way to disciple is to love others and point them to Jesus to encounter Him personally in relationship.

It's important to remember that good discipleship will always be all about Jesus. Ultimately, we are discipled by the Holy Spirit, as Jesus' promise in John 14:26 describes, "But the Advocate, the Holy Spirit, whom the Father will send in my name, will teach you all things and will remind you of everything I have said to you." As the Holy Spirit teaches and disciples us, He also wants us to be discipled by other believers and disciple other believers ourselves.

Invitation to Journey Deeper:

- Who has discipled you in your faith journey? How can you practice being a disciple?
- If you do not have a spiritual mentor, who could ask to join you on your faith journey?

For Further Reading: 1 Corinthians 11:1

PRACTISING
DISCIPLESHIP

As believers, it is critical that we engage in the process of discipleship. Jesus declares in Mark 1:17, "'Come, follow Me... and I will send you out to fish for people.'" In other words, when we commit to following Jesus, we are committing to both being discipled and becoming a discipler.

By practising discipleship through following Jesus' teachings, we will know Him better and declare to the world that we are His followers. Our lives and love will be a declaration of His love for others and invite them to know God the way we know Him.

Before His ascension, Jesus delivered a final charge to His followers in the Great Commission: "All authority in heaven and on earth has been given to Me. Therefore go and make disciples of all nations, baptizing them in the name of the Father and of the Son and of the Holy Spirit, and teaching them to obey everything I have commanded you. And surely I am with you always, to the very end of the age" (Matthew 28:18-20).

In this, we are called to make disciples of all nations, teaching and guiding as Scripture declares and as the Spirit leads. Jesus teaches people, teaches people to teach people, and teaches people how to teach people. Or, as Paul explains in 2 Timothy 2:2, "...the things you have heard me say in the presence of many witnesses entrust to reliable people who will also be qualified to teach others." The cascade of discipleship from Paul to Timothy to "reliable" people eventually, through the centuries, has carried down to Christians in discipleship today. It is our responsibility to carry the torch on.

SETTING THE PRISONERS FREE

So if the Son sets you free, you will be free indeed.

—John 8:36

Once Jesus sets you free, the world will notice. I will never forget a friend coming up to me after I had spent a week with a ministry called *Restoring the Foundations,* which focuses on inner healing, generational issues, strongholds, ungodly beliefs, soul ties, and deliverance.[1] "What happened to you? You are full of life and light!" she exclaimed. This woman was deeply involved in the New Age Movement and was spiritually sensitive. She could tell that my countenance had changed. She could tell I had a new lease on life. Jesus' healing touch changed my spirit, stature, and attitude in ways that were noticeable to everyone.

God loves everyone and has a plan for all! No one is here by accident. Submission to Jesus puts you back in alignment with God's ultimate and beautiful plan for your life and the redemption of the world.

Jesus trained His disciples to set people free because God's will is for us to be liberated from whatever bondage we are in and to go and liberate others.

What does it mean to be free? How do you become free?

When we accept Jesus and are born again, we enter into a process of sanctification (the process of being set apart and made holy as we become more like Christ). As we surrender more and more of our lives to He who reigns, we experience the relief that comes from knowing the Creator of the universe is once again on the throne of our lives. Sin no longer binds us or ties us to the world through His grace. In Christ, we are new creations, once again connected to the Father, made whole and complete in Him.

I have been crucified with Christ and I no longer live, but Christ lives in me. The life I now live in the body, I live by faith in the Son of God, who loved me and gave Himself for me.

—*Galatians 2:20*

The enemy will try to keep us in the dark about the fact that we were crucified with Christ and our former self is dead. The religious spirit will portray an angry God who demands constant "penance," or self-inflicted guilt, payback, and punishment.[2] The Greek word for repentance is *metanoia*, which refers to a "change of mind." In other words, it is godly sorrow because we love God. We must continually renew our minds in the process of sanctification to fully grasp the reality and manifest the life of Jesus. We can only be as free as the depth of our surrender and our co-inclusion with Jesus.

Invitation to Journey Deeper:

- What areas of your life does God want to set you free from?
- How are Christians expected to live differently in the world?

For Further Reading: Galatians 5:13 and 2 Corinthians 3:17

---

1. Learn more about Restoring the Foundations at https://www.restoringthefoundations.org.
2. See pages 82-95 for more on the religious spirit.

BLINDED BY THE AGE

For their minds have been blinded by the god of this age, leaving them in unbelief. Their blindness keeps them from seeing the dayspring light of the gospel of the glory of Christ, who is the divine image of God.

—2 Corinthians 4:4, TPT

We are born knowing right and wrong. God imprints His moral code into our hearts. Our conscience knows we are sinners and tells us we are accountable to our Creator. Over time, if we choose to continually disobey our conscience, it will become hardened, and our inner voice of truth is lost, desensitised, and corrupted. In his second letter to the Corinthians, Paul writes that the god of this age is Satan, who blinds people from receiving the good news of the gospel.

A corrupted conscience perceives good as evil and evil as good. It results in "truth" becoming relative and self-determined. Of course, a corrupted conscience is blind to this reality, and tragically, our culture, education systems, media, and entertainment bombard us with content that corrupts and desensitises our conscience daily.

Those aware of their sinful nature, brokenness, and weakness are prepared to receive the gospel. Jesus came to save those who know they have a problem, not those who claim to be righteous. We must admit that we need a saviour, and that requires repentance. To turn from our old ways and towards God results in godly thinking.

Jesus answered them, "It is not the healthy who need a doctor, but the sick. I have not come to call the righteous, but sinners to repentance."

—Luke 5:31-32

Jesus loved those rejected by the world with compassion and mercy. He was ridiculed for spending time with prostitutes, tax collectors, the unlovable and the unacceptable... everyone who was rejected by the self-righteous Pharisees whose hearts were hardened by the Law.[1] It is legalism that robs faith of its power and provokes punishment. Everyone is sick. Some self-righteously *think* they are healthy.

Satan, the god of this age, comes to steal, kill, and destroy through secrecy, ignorance, deception, and division. But, thankfully, as 1 John 1:9 explains, "If we confess our sins, He is faithful and just and will forgive us our sins and purify us from all unrighteousness."

Remember: God convicts us of sin to draw us back to Him. Conviction moves us towards God and His healing. Condemnation pushes us to hide and drown in guilt and shame. Condemnation is demonic, intending to keep us from experiencing God. The next time you feel a prick of "I did something wrong," ask the Holy Spirit to show you whether you are feeling conviction or condemnation. He will show you what to do next.

Invitation to Journey Deeper:

- Ask the Holy Spirit, in what ways am I blinded by the world?
- Surrender what He shows you and place your focus back on Jesus.

For Further Reading: Romans 4:14-15

---

1. For more on the Law, see the page 68.

DETHRONED

"Be perfect, therefore, as your heavenly Father is perfect."

—Matthew 5:48

How many times in our lives have we broken God's standard? Lying, cheating, stealing, having hate in your heart, lustful thoughts or sex before marriage, using the Lord's name in vain... the list of sins is endless. God sees everything we do, think, and feel, and there is no way to hide from Him.

> *The heart is deceitful above all things and beyond cure. Who can understand it? "I the Lord search the heart and examine the mind, to reward each person according to their conduct, according to what their deeds deserve."*

—Jeremiah 17:9-10

The suffering and darkness in the world make it clear that we all need a saviour... *the* Saviour. We deceive ourselves if we think we are without sin. The fallen human race requires the grace of God to be made into new creations with new natures. This is why I am a Christian.

The point is that we are all desperately guilty, and we get off the hook by pleading guilty!

Only Jesus lived a perfect life. Salvation comes with a humbled heart that is repentant to God through faith in Jesus. By God's grace, our Saviour closed the sin-induced gap between man and God by coming to earth to do what we could never do on our own—present a perfect and final sacrifice for sin. We are all born sinners who will come face-to-face with a Holy God one day. To make Jesus our Lord and Saviour, we must humble ourselves and repent (i.e., dethrone ourselves). I have tried to find peace in this world, and let me tell you, the incredible freedom, peace, and joy that awaits you on the other side of submission is unimaginable!

It is prideful to have confidence in our ability to fulfil God's Law, which demands absolute morality with absolute perfection. Jesus says in Mark 10:18, "No one is good—except God alone." Dos and don'ts, rules or formulas, false religions (including works based on "karmic" Christianity, being a "good person," etc.), *anything* relying on our own strength, is religion. If we choose the Law, the standard is absolute perfection. It feeds our pride and removes our dependence on God, the source of our strength and Redeemer who makes all things new. The greater our bondage to religion, the further we get from the genuine relationship God wants with us.

Today and every day, I choose to submit my life and my will to God. This puts me in a place of receiving, not achieving. Being yoked to Jesus and having found rest for my soul, I am empowered to live righteously by grace. Being the lord of my own life was terrible. I can't imagine ever living like that again. I am so thankful that I am no longer on the throne of my life.

Invitation to Journey Deeper:

- Who is on the throne of your life? What areas have you been unwilling to submit to God?
- What role does repentance play in your daily life? What is God calling you to repent from today?
- Spend time in prayer asking the Holy Spirit for wisdom and strength to become more like Jesus every day.
- Close your eyes and imagine yourself sitting on the throne of your own life. Now stand up, get off the throne and invite Jesus to take your place. What happens next?

For Further Reading: Ephesians 2:8

THE OLD COVENANT
and the NEW COVENANT

The Old Covenant refers to God's physical, earthly agreement with His people, the children of Israel. Under this agreement, God promised the Israelites that they would be blessed because of their obedience to His law and through a system of animal sacrifices to atone for their sins. The Old Covenant lasted for hundreds of years.

As Jesus prophesied in Mark 13, the temple where animals were sacrificed was destroyed, and with it, the system God's children once needed to be made right with Him. Thankfully, through the death and resurrection of Jesus, the ultimate and final sacrifice, we are now the temple of the Holy Spirit, and Jesus serves as our superior and eternal High Priest. We have entered into the New Covenant.

The New Covenant is the spiritual agreement outlined in Matthew 5 - 7. This agreement is not contrary to the Law, but the fulfillment of the Old Covenant, and those who submit to it through surrender to Jesus are promised spiritual and physical blessings, eternal life, and the gift of the Holy Spirit.

Throughout the Old Testament, or the scriptural books written during the Old Covenant, God says clearly over and over that a New Covenant is coming. This new agreement will fulfil God's promise to put His law on our hearts, put His Spirit within us, and help us to walk in His ways through the help of the Messiah. Through the New Covenant, our relationship with God is restored once and for all because of the freedom we gain in His sacrifice!

The Old and New Covenants are not at odds with each other. Rather, the Old Covenant was made knowing that the New was coming. There would be no New Covenant without the Old. And without the promise of the New Covenant, the Old Covenant is meaningless. Through Jesus' sacrifice, God displays His faithfulness to His people and the world. He sent His Messiah as promised, perfectly fulfilling the Old Covenant and paving the way for our adoption as His children.

A few of the key differences between the Old and New Covenants include:

Old Covenant	New Covenant
Holy Spirit given only to aselect few for specific periods of time (Numbers 27:18)	Holy Spirit given to all (Romans 7:6)
A High Priest (man) was required to serve as mediator between God and man (Exodus 28:29-30)	Jesus, perfect and sinless, is our perpetual High Priest (Hebrews 4:14-16)
Animal sacrifice to pay for sins (Leviticus 1-7)	Jesus is the ultimate sacrifice (Hebrews 10:14-17)

Old Covenant	New Covenant
Imperative to keep the Law to the letter (Leviticus 1-7)	Bearing the fruit of the Spirit and good works are required (Galatians 5:22 - 24)
Between God and the children of Israel (Genesis 26:3)	Between God and those who accept the gift of salvation through His Son. (Acts 10:34-43)
Exposes sin (Galatians 3:19)	Removes our sin as far as the east is from the west (Psalm 103:12; Romans 4:7-8)
Cannot give life (2 Corinthians 3:7)	Gives life (Galatians 3:11)
Brings a curse (Galatians 3:10)	Redeemed from the curse (Galatians 3:13)

FROM BONDAGE TO FREEDOM

Then you will know the truth, and the truth will set you free.

—John 8:32

Jesus is the truth. If He sets you free, you will be free indeed. To be totally free, we must tear down everything in our lives that opposes the will of God and replace those things with the truth. What exactly are the things that we need to be freed from?

- Self (our carnal mind, self-focus, desires, ways, and independence)
- Participation in the occult (this relates to idolatry, freemasonry, yoga, and being a victim of the occult)
- Deception (self-deception, blindness, denial, or minimising the truth)
- Performance (through comparison, competition, people-pleasing, striving, religious performance, or self-sufficiency)
- Suppressed or blocked emotions, unresolved heart/soul issues, abandonment, rejection, neglect, victimisation, trauma/wounds, and shame (resulting from guilt, regret, self-accusation, or sexual sins)
- Insecurity, fear, and control (manifested through appeasement, denial, a false sense of responsibility, enabling, pride, or controlling others through anger)
- Religion (the Law, sin-consciousness, obligation, or performance)

The above list includes some of the things Jesus set me free from.[1] I've engaged in emotional and heart-healing in my quiet times with the Lord, with different ministries, and with believing counsellors to help me work through generational issues, soul ties, strongholds, deliverance, etc. But of course, there are many more areas of life that hold people in bondage, and areas of my heart and life God continues to reveal and set me from from as I give them over to Him. Jesus' blood sets us free as we appropriate His victory in every area of our lives. It is no longer we who live but Christ who lives in us! Jesus paid the full price for the past, present, and all of eternity. This is grace. That He is our righteousness, holiness, love, joy, peace, and freedom. Grace empowers us through God's love to not sin. When we receive the revelation of Jesus' grace, our motivation to live a godly lifestyle overflows out of love, not condemnation or obligation. As Romans 8:1 declares, "Therefore, there is now no condemnation for those who are in Christ Jesus."

Invitation to Journey Deeper:

- In what areas of your life are you relying on your own strength?
- What bondage do you need to be set free from? Ask the Lord to reveal any hidden areas. Consider reaching out to a pastor, deliverance ministry, believing counsellor, mentor, or friend for more serious areas. This may be the first step towards a process of healing meant to be done with the support of a community of believers.

For Further Reading: John 8:36 and Galatians 2:20

---

1. The list of occult activities listed in this reflection require repentance, renounce-ment, and deliverance in order to be set free. If you have participated in any of the activities listed, I strongly encourage you to seek out a Spirit-filled inner-healing and deliverance ministry to help you with the process.

DELIVERANCE

Jesus said, "Let the little children come to Me, and do not hinder them, for the Kingdom of heaven belongs to such as these."

—Matthew 19:14

Jesus tells us that we will not enter His Kingdom unless we become like children. To be childlike is to become humble, innocent, and teachable. A child is open and trusting, seeking to understand with awe and wonder. Children ask many questions with expectancy and long for love and guidance.

While I became a Christian at a young age and was raised in a Christian home, I did not experience the full freedom Jesus offered until I surrendered my life to Him with childlike faith and trust. As we come to the Lord like children, embracing a lifestyle of repentance and sanctification, we will experience greater levels of freedom. The sooner we repent, the less we will have to deal with the effects of sin, and the doors sin opens to the demonic world. Repentance should be a regular part of our lifestyle as believers, as the truth delivers us from old or inferior mindsets. This renewing of our mind awakens us to see ourselves in Him. The truth sets us free!

The enemy requires agreement to operate in our lives. Deliverance organically occurs as we align our thinking with the truth, replacing lies and ungodly beliefs; address oppression, taking authority over any demonic spirits; and break agreements with the enemy. No doubt, there are multiple potential causes for the struggles we face, and God uses medicine, therapists, situations, people, natural remedies, etc., to comfort and heal. However, deliverance and inner-healing is required for spiritual struggles that no amount of counselling, medication, exercise, or self-help can fix.[1]

These issues include things like but are not limited to poverty, religion, failure, pride, sickness, trauma, mental illness, deception, addiction, substance abuse, involvement in evil/secret societies, ungodly beliefs, soul ties, hurts, unresolved anger, family history, or lack of mercy. At its core, it involves anything that keeps you in bondage to the enemy and prevents you from living a full, joyful, healthy life. However, *Jesus can set you free from all of these things forever.*

God has not only healed me but He has set me free from experiences and memories that held me back, and now I can press on knowing God is with me always. And we know that where the Spirit of the Lord is, there is freedom! All we have to do is trust Him like a little child, knowing He is a good and faithful Father.

Invitation to Journey Deeper:

- What memories or experiences does Jesus want to deliver and heal you from? Who can you reach out to for prayer over these areas?
- What would it feel like to be set free from the chains of the enemy?

For Further Reading: Psalm 144:2; 3:3 and 2 Corinthians 3:17

---

1. Soul (mind, will, and emotion) care is critical as is our physical health. However, we must be aware of the spiritual forces at play. Emotional traumas are open doors that must be healed.

JESUS SET ME FREE

By the grace of God, Jesus delivered me from two of the most traumatic memories of my life.

_____

When my brother was just 13 years old, he accidentally shot himself in the head. For years, the gruesome memory of me holding my brother's head with a towel as his body convulsed on the floor was burnt in my mind. Now, I see Jesus beside my brother, holding his hand after the accident. He was right there with us.

Then as an adult, I imagined the horror Abbe faced on the night of her death as more details emerged about her tragic end. My oldest daughter brutally slashed and stabbed, with the fatal wound a stab in her heart.

In time, Jesus showed me that He was there in the midst of this hellish situation. Now, I see my daughter, safely at home with Jesus in a new body.

_____

The enemy could have continued to use those memories to torture me and hold me in bondage to trauma and pain. (In fact, he did for nearly 32 years after my brother's accident.) But by abiding in Him, engaging with the Holy Spirit in my prayer time or in prayer times with others, Jesus stepped in and literally re-worked my memories. In their place, Jesus set me free, brought inner healing to my heart that only He can do, and gave me glorious new visions of His truth and mercy.

CONTENDING FOR FREEDOM

At last we have freedom, for Christ has set us free! We must always cherish this truth and firmly refuse to go back into the bondage of our past.

—Galatians 5:1, TPT

Jesus may ask you to contend for your freedom, alone or with others. There was a time when a wonderful group of believers prayed and fasted for 28 days over my daughter, Bryn. Following Abbe's death, Bryn woke up every morning screaming and crying that she wanted to die in the midst of drug addiction, depression, and grappling with the deep scars left by repeated sexual abuse by someone who was once close to our family.

By His grace, God set Bryn free from the spirit of death (forever!) at a deliverance session. There is a moment that stands out to us when we both realised those dark, terrifying days were coming to an end. On the way home from a deliverance session, I moved too quickly into another lane on the highway, and Bryn called out, "Dad, be careful! I don't want to die!"

Bryn and I both went silent, then looked at each other and laughed in shock. *My daughter didn't want to die. She wanted to live! Jesus had set her free from the spirit of death!* To this day, she has never been the same. And at the time of writing this book, Bryn serves full-time at a missionary base in Hawaii.

This started a new process of progressive freedom and relationship for Bryn. Jesus stepped in and transformed her life to one on fire for Him, full of life and joy. She embraces abundant life, increasing in truth and freedom more and more each day.

The point is, becoming a Christian is about so much more than securing your "ticket to heaven." Instead, Jesus wants you free to live a full, beautiful, profoundly powerful life that brings healing and freedom to others.

Repentance is about reconciling our relationship with God. Repentance is a lifestyle of renewing our mind (changing our thinking), and Jesus offers it to us daily. I love repentance because I have experienced the fruit of turning from sin and towards Jesus so many times in my life. When something surfaces, through His grace, I repent, renounce, receive forgiveness, declare the truth, and choose to realign that area of my life with Jesus because I desire to protect our relationship. Once again, I choose to agree with God's ways, to think like Him and awaken to the truth of who I am in Christ and the power of His blood. This process constantly refocuses me on the things above. It helps me not get distracted by my physical circumstances or allow a wedge to come in between God and me. By His grace, I am not subject to the wages of sin. I get to experience the gift of eternal life in Him!

I do not want to revert to my old ways. I repent to return to the innocence of my new nature that Jesus purchased. I want to stay free and progressively become freer by renewing my mind to the truth! We are already perfected in Christ and must awaken to this reality. I never want to be bound to anything or anyone other than Jesus ever again. When I receive greater freedom, I can freely give to others. What I overcome through Christ's power in me, I have authority over.

I hope that my story and what I've learnt will inspire and ignite a hunger in you to pursue Jesus for yourself. I pray that you would experience the freedom He has for you by constantly receiving the truth of God's Word and learning to apply the victory of Jesus to every area of your life. In Christ, we are free. We have the Holy Spirit and where the Spirit of the Lord is, there is freedom. As Jesus proclaimed, it is finished!

Invitation to Journey Deeper:

- Repentance is a daily choice to turn from our old ways and choose Jesus. Looking back, how have you grown in Christ-likeness?
- What area of your life is God calling you to contend for? Pause and ask the Lord to search your heart.
- Is there someone else in your life God is calling you to contend for? Take time to pray for clarity in this area.

For Further Reading: Romans 6:23

THE RELIGIOUS SPIRIT AND THE COUNTERFEIT

*I have been crucified with Christ and I no longer live, but Christ lives
in me. The life I now live in the body, I live by faith in the Son of God,
who loved me and gave Himself for me.*

—*Galatians* 2:20

Christianity is technically a religion in that it is an organised set of
beliefs focused on worshipping a god or gods (in this case, the one true
God). However, it is much more than that. As believers, we know that
Christianity is more than a set of rules, rituals, traditions, or even what
you choose to believe. While belief in Jesus is the only way to receive
eternal life, God is really after a relationship with us. It's when we get
stuck on "religion" (the Law) and forget about having a relationship
with God our Father that we really get into trouble. Jesus did not come
to create a Christian "religion" but to fully reveal God and redeem all
of creation, defeating sin once and for all.

Jesus' death on the cross and resurrection fulfilled the Law, transferring
His righteousness to us by grace through faith. His blood paid the full
price that we could never pay because no human being could ever fully
fulfil the Law.

When I first tried bringing Christianity into my company, it was more
religion-focused than relationship-focused because I was religious (not
the pure, unblemished religion Paul writes about in Galatians, but the
legalistic, religious spirit that condemns). The result was a tense, exclu-
sive, and even "weird" culture. It definitely did not draw people into
God's Kingdom. However, as I matured in Christ and grew to understand the gospel of grace, everything changed. Now we are actually a
"Kingdom-company," and it is incredible! Kingdom culture works
everywhere. The difference is operating out of our sonship versus
striving as orphans.

The religious spirit replaces relationship with works and wars against the operation of grace in our lives. It makes love conditional and earned. The religious spirit feasts on the Tree of Knowledge of Good and Evil (the Law), leading to death and separating us from God, whereas Jesus is the Tree of Life (grace). When you feel offense, judgement, self-condemnation, exhaustion, emptiness, or accusation in your heart, and your experience of God or reading the Word is more of a grind, you have probably allowed the spirit of religion to enter.

I attended a conference once where a Christian leader shared a word from the Lord. "The Lord wants you to sit on His lap, and He wants to tickle you!" Half of the room broke out into laughter. The other half turned sour and judgemental. While the word may have offended some religious people, the reality is that heaven is filled with laughter and joy, and it is our Father's desire to fill us with His laughter and joy, too.

If the truth resides only in our minds as "head knowledge," it can easily become legalistic and religious—like the Pharisees. The spirit of religion is Satan's counterfeit of the real thing. It steals the joy of our relationship with God. Thankfully, the cross plundered the religious spirit of its authority. We do not have to live under its heavy yoke! Jesus fulfilled the Law on our behalf with His blood. It is finished! Grace through faith in Jesus opens our consciousness to the truth of our new creation life. His righteousness is now ours, once and for all.

Invitation to Journey Deeper:

- When, where, or how have you fallen into the "religion" trap? What were the consequences?
- Why are legalism and head knowledge often easier to rely on for truth?
- How is God calling you to experience more of His goodness?

For Further Reading: James 1:27 and Isaiah 29:13

SPIRIT OF RELIGION?

There are many reasons why people get trapped in a lifestyle or mindset of "religion" versus having a true relationship with God. I once heard someone refer to Christians stuck in the spirit of religion as "imprisoned royalty," operating from a false reality and false identity.

For some reason, we think we are "good enough" and deserve to go to heaven on our own merit. Here is the truth: We don't deserve heaven and have no part in our salvation, but God's love made the way through faith alone. This gift of grace may be hard to comprehend, but it is one we all need to receive. If you don't know that you are God's beloved child, it is easy to think you have to perform for His love. I know I did. Even if you don't think you are practising your faith out of the spirit of religion, it never hurts to pause and search your heart for any wrong motive in your actions or decision-making. Take a few moments to read through the questions below as you check in with your spirit and ask God to reveal the condition of your heart.

- Do you feel like you will be punished if you make a mistake?

- Do you struggle to believe God is infinitely good and loves and accepts you unconditionally?

- Do you feel like you are falling short?

- Are you stuck or chained to the past?

- Are you a Christian and do not experience peace, joy, and freedom from a relationship with Jesus?

- Have you ever felt disqualified?

- Are you insecure and fearful?

- Does faith feel like a burden?

- Do you feel burnt out in life?

- Are you trapped in performance-based living?

- Is your value or identity based on what you do rather than who God says you are?

- Have you ever felt like there's a punisher standing on your shoulder?

- Have you ever felt like your heart is accusing you or condemning you?

- Is it difficult to rest in the presence of the Lord?

- When you see someone living in sin, do you feel led to condemn, shame, and compare?

- Do you find it hard to receive God's forgiveness or forgive others?

- Do you tend to over-spiritualise everything?

- Do you feel like you have to act and look a certain way?

- Is it difficult to hear the voice of God?

- Do you dwell on right or wrong (in yourself, others, and the world)?

- Are you motivated by fear of punishment instead of God's love?

If you answered "yes" to any of these questions, you are likely living out some aspect of your faith in the spirit of religion and/or simply not receiving God's truth. This is thinking as an orphan (not a child of God) due to operating out of a false identity. You can see how orphans and the religious spirit go hand in hand.

Remember, God loves and accepts you just as you are, but He won't leave you as you are! He wants a heart-level relationship with you! He's not worried about you being perfect or getting it right every time. It's not up to you to make sure everyone else gets it right every time, either. The religious spirit makes God's love conditional, requiring one to earn it. This is a total lie. When we receive His unconditional love, we experience true rest, peace, and joy.

RELIGION VS. RELATIONSHIP

Love is patient, love is kind. It does not envy, it does not boast, it is not proud.

—1 Corinthians 13:4

A religious spirit can slowly choke out the Kingdom of righteousness and our peace and joy in the Holy Spirit if we choose to agree with it. A religious spirit can seep in anywhere, especially impacting our relationships and union with God and His people. Jesus offers a relational theology, meaning everything in the Kingdom flows from relationships (the chief purpose of theology is to know God). All God requires is faith (again, our job is to believe) as faith accesses His righteousness and His Kingdom.

In the church, the religious spirit often shows up as pride in people-pleasing (fear of man) or unresolved heart issues. This usually binds people to the chains of "niceness," manifesting itself in masks, fakeness, inauthenticity, and disconnection. To be "nice" is to act pleasant and agreeable. Nice people don't make waves. They don't enter into conflict out of fear. They don't call others out for unacceptable behaviour. I have seen this happen in my company and my family, so it is not an issue unique to the church.

Niceness hides. It doesn't say the difficult things that need to be said. Niceness is a form of people-pleasing, a facade, and doesn't ask the hard questions. Niceness doesn't hold others to a high standard. It placates, promotes weakness, and allows mediocrity. Niceness creates a false peace, making true unity impossible.

In contrast, kindness emerges from love (which is a fruit of the Spirit and enables others to bear good fruit). Kindness speaks the truth and is unwavering. Kindness is both humble and courageous. It is generous, it is transparent, it is thoughtful and considerate. Kindness says difficult things constructively, embraces conflict to a better end, and takes the initiative because it cares. Kindness holds others to a higher standard, is accountable, provides direct, honest feedback, and serves others. Kindness is authentic, passionate, and rooted in integrity and excellence. Kindness results in genuine connection and unity. Pretending to be kind is a lie. Honest communication is the key to freedom because the truth sets us free.

We cannot make our old nature holy. It is dead. Religion, legalism, and fear of punishment all go hand in hand. Each only produces orphans. A religious spirit is in the head (knowledge of God), whereas Jesus is in the heart (revelation and relationship with God).

We are not called to religion. We are not called to be nice. We are called to true relationships, to pure, unblemished faith in Jesus. And we are called to be kind. There is a great difference between religiosity and relationship and between niceness and kindness. Jesus was never nice. He was *always* kind. So be free, honest, authentic, and kind like Jesus; discard your mask (and religion) and be you! Where the Spirit of the Lord is, there is freedom!

Invitation to Journey Deeper:

- Explain the difference between being nice and being kind in your own words. How have you mistaken the two in the past?
- How is God asking you to be kind in light of the gospel?
- Why do you think it feels easier to default to "nice" mode?

For Further Reading: 2 Corinthians 3:17 and Ephesians 1:5

WHAT IS THE
SPIRIT OF RELIGION?

- Religion (i.e., the spirit of religion) is man's attempt to approach God in his own strength and performance. It is a form of godliness with no power, an outside-in attempt at transformation.

- Religion cannot produce life; it cannot be the solution to the problems it creates.

- Religion makes it about our ability, not God's ability.

- Religion attempts to add to the cross as if Christ's sacrifice were not enough.

- Religion lies and says you need to earn and perform your way to God's love.

- Religion is bondage as it cannot accept the fullness of grace that comes from receiving through faith alone.

- Religion evokes our old nature separated from God.

- Religion confuses identity with behaviour.

- Religion can only produce orphans dependent on themselves. Orphans are predisposed to acting out of the religious spirit to receive acceptance.

THE SPIRIT OF RELIGION

IN THE CHURCH

Unsurprisingly, the religious spirit is prevalent in the church, as evidenced by the reality that many churches are places where doctrine, rules, judgement, performance, and earning have replaced the extravagant gospel of grace, the good news of God's love.

"The chief danger of the 20th century will be religion without the Holy Spirit, Christianity without repentance, salvation without regeneration, politics without God and heaven without hell." —William Booth*

Legalism and the religious spirit (a sure sign our flesh or old nature is active) can quickly bind us to rituals, performance, dos and don'ts, pride, and shame— all of which are entirely opposed to the message of Christ's death on the cross. How so? Any system that encourages us to rely on our own strength, traditions, or history instead of relying on the saving power of Jesus is a system that leads to death.

He alone makes us adequate ministers who are focused on an entirely new covenant. Our ministry is not based on the letter of the law but through the power of the Spirit. The letter of the law kills, but the Spirit pours out life. —2 Corinthians 3:6, TPT

Remember, works do not please God. Our job is to submit ourselves to Christ, following His command to love God first, and second to love our neighbor as ourselves. It's that simple!

*"William Booth Quotes," Goodreads, accessed November 23, 2021, https://www.goodreads.com/quotes/792960-the-chief-danger-of-the-20th-century-will-be-religion

OUT OF THE BOX GOD

The Lord, the Lord, the compassionate and gracious God, slow to anger, abounding in love and faithfulness...

—Exodus 34:6

The way we see God work in our lives reflects how we view God. If we view God as the all-powerful, wonder-working, miracle-making Creator of the universe, we will see His fingerprints on every area of our lives.

> "Our image (concept) of God is the most important thing about us. It determines our relationship with God, others, and ourselves. Many people we talk with need healing in their image of God. Do you? Your answer to this question will tell you: Can you look back over your whole life and say, 'My Father God has always been good to me.'? If not, your heart is hurting and your image of God needs healing."
>
> —Bill Gaultiere[1]

Below you will find a list of lies that we are all tempted to believe about God at times. These lies can seem to make sense regarding God's existence and the reason for our suffering. However, when our experiences become the bottom line in our theologies, we put God in a box, ignore Scripture, and are in danger of heresy. Consider the following lies:

- *God doesn't heal anymore.*
- *God isn't interested in my everyday life.*
- *I can't hear God. God only speaks through the Bible; He no longer speaks directly to His people.*
- *No one could ever love me. I am not enough. I am not worthy.*
- *No one could ever rescue me from my hopeless circumstances!*

Most likely, you resonated with at least one of those statements. Not one is true, but they certainly can feel true at times. Why is that? Ultimately, it is because when we put limits on our relationship with God, we are the ones responsible. We are the ones putting God in a box, not the other way around.

> The trajectory of your whole life is determined by one single thing; the image of God that you live your life with. Sadly, most people live with a false view of God; that He is irrelevant, critical, distant and not very interesting. It's a lie. It is a tragedy to live with a false view of God, it effects everything in your life.
>
> —Doug Sherman[2]

I used to see God through my human understanding and resonated with many of the previous statements. The result was that my view of God was small and limited. Today, I know the truth of our unseeable, supreme, unimaginable, and inexpressible God. He sits on His throne and laughs at the enemy's schemes, and so should we since we sit with Jesus in heavenly places.

Invitation to Journey Deeper:

- What is your view of God? How have you limited Him?
- Which statement listed did you resonate with most? Why?

For Further Reading: Ephesians 2:6 and John 14:6

———————————————————————

1. "Bible Verses on the Father's Love," *Soul Shepherding*, accessed November 23, 2021, https://www.soulshepherding.org/bible-verses-on-the-fathers-love/.
2. Doug Sherman, "About Doug Sherman," TradingUp.org, Accessed July 11, 2022, https://www.tradingup.org/site/about/doug.

A GOD WITHOUT LIMITS

Never doubt God's mighty power to work in you and accomplish all this. He will achieve infinitely more than your greatest request, your most unbelievable dream, and exceed your wildest imagination!

—*Ephesians 3:20a, TPT*

After my brother's accident, my family, friends, and church spent much time praying for his healing over many years. Prophets and pastors came to my brother's bedside and then left. Unfortunately, he did not receive healing and passed away after living 25 years in a declining vegetative state. This experience impacted my ability to see God as a healer.

At the same time, I also struggled to believe that God was relational and wanted to know me. I knew He was the Creator, but a part of me always worried that some new scientific discovery would prove me wrong. All of that began to change when Bryn and I stayed with my mother in New Brunswick just before she had a very difficult stint in rehab. My mother took us to visit with a gathering of believers for a simple evening worship service. I sat in the back, listening quietly. It had been a tough season with my struggling daughters, and I was exhausted.

The pastor kept looking at me throughout worship. Turns out, the Lord had given him a powerful prophetic word over my life. Finally, he stopped the service and spoke out about what God had shown him about Bryn and me. As he and other believers spoke, many of the boxes I had surrounding God's character began to break. God saw me and knew me. He knew me intimately and had shared details of my life and my daughter's life with a group of strangers. It was a life-changing moment for both of us. My journey towards a deeper connection with Jesus had begun as God connected me with His body in a new way.

Our God can do far more than we could imagine. However, our lives do not always reflect that reality. The reason is that our lack of faith can actually block what God wants to do. We are all guilty of putting God in one box or another at some point in our lives. When God does not answer a prayer the way we want Him to, when a painful circumstance sideswipes us, or when we are faced with the realities of living in a fallen world, we are all too quick to build a theology about God around our experience. To break out of such limiting mindsets, we must come face-to-face with the unimaginable immensity of our awesome God. And the best place to start is the Bible.

Not long after my prophetic experience at the worship night (we eventually all became great friends), I read the Bible from Genesis to Revelation in a year. If you want to know who God is and what He does, read His Word. Nothing challenges boxes like the truth. I now read the Bible every day to remind myself that our God is without limits. Our God is an Ephesians 3:20 God!

Invitation to Journey Deeper:

- Do you believe God is relational? What words would you use to describe your relationship with God?
- How familiar with God's Word are you?
- Do you spend time regularly reading and meditating on God's Word? If so, how has it impacted your walk with the Lord? If not, when and how can you incorporate this into your days?

For Further Reading: Romans 5:11

BECOMING AND BEHOLDING

And so we know and rely on the love God has for us. God is love. Whoever lives in love lives in God, and God in them.

—1 John 4:16

We become like the one we behold and what we hold in our hearts will have expression on the earth. For example, if we focus on things that make us anxious, we will become anxious. If we keep our eyes on Jesus, we become like Him as our mind renews to the truth of our identity in Him. What is true in Him is true in us! As we abide and live in union with Jesus, His nature becomes our nature. When Jesus was on earth, He only did what He saw the Father doing and only said what He heard the Father saying. In His perfect obedience, Jesus became like the Father. What's more, we are made in God's image, and Jesus is the perfect image of God. As such, the more we become like Jesus, the more we become as God intended us to be before the fall of man.

1 Corinthians 13:4-8 beautifully describes God's nature as demonstrated through Jesus, the perfect visible image of our invisible God. If we replace the word "love" with "Father" in this passage (because God is love), we see His true nature coming alive:

> *Our Father is patient, our Father is kind. He does not envy, He does not boast, He is not proud. He does not dishonor others, He is not self-seeking, He is not easily angered, He keeps no record of wrongs. Our Father does not delight in evil but rejoices with the truth. Our Father always protects, always trusts, always hopes, always perseveres.*

I don't know about you, but I don't know anyone who meets the standard of love set by our Father. Let's behold our Father!

How has spending time with Jesus changed me? The peace I experience is the peace that Jesus says in Philippians 4:7 " ...transcends all understanding...." I regularly experience peace even in the darkest of times, from my daughter's murder trial to life and hardships in business. He has my life, and I trust my Dad, my eternal heavenly Father. This is true inexpressible freedom. I have come to a point where I often feel the love of God for the one in front of me, which was previously not my default. Today, I can confidently say that He is the source of my strength and resiliency. His Holy Spirit living in me gives me encouragement, hope, endurance, truth, perseverance, support, and strength. In other words, focusing on Jesus has changed everything. I am a completely different person, and that is a very good thing. I am coming into a greater consciousness of my union with Jesus, safe and secure, a son who is one with God. Christ in me is the hope of glory.

Invitation to Journey Deeper:

Set aside some time to journal through the following questions. The answers will prove insightful to who you are and who you are becoming:

1. What do you want most?
2. What fills the majority of your thought-life?
3. What do you spend your money on?
4. How do you spend your free time?
5. Who do you like to spend time with?
6. Who do you admire most?

What themes do you see when you read over your answers? What season is God calling you into? Is there anything He wants you to turn from? The more time you spend with Him, the more you will become like Him and see where He is leading you.

For Further Reading: Genesis 1:27 and 1 John 4:16

NO OTHER NAME

Salvation is found in no one else, for there is no other name under heaven given to mankind by which we must be saved.

—Acts 4:12

The Bible talks about how the "sons of God," the created gods, *elohim* or spirit beings, rebelled to become the powers and principalities of darkness in high places. These beings are very real; however, there is no other god above our God. No other god who calls himself our father and us, his beloved children. There is only one uncreated being.

For even if there are so-called gods, whether in heaven or on earth (as indeed there are many "gods" and many "lords"), yet for us there is but one God, the Father, from whom all things came and for whom we live; and there is but one Lord, Jesus Christ, through whom all things came and through whom we live.

—1 Corinthians 8:5-6

Many fallen beings make up the gods of this world and are the basis for many myths and pagan religions. Unfortunately, many are unaware that these spirits can plant thoughts in our minds (which we often mistake for our own thoughts). Of course, these deceiving voices are not just behind other religions but are often behind political or philosophical ideologies. Take humanism.[1] It sounds noble at first glance, but once you start digging, you'll discover that humanism is entirely void of godliness and, as such, is deception. Beware of "isms."

While many knowingly or unknowingly worship fallen, dead, or created beings in pagan religions, others do not believe in the supernatural or the spirit realm at all. This alternative deception is exactly what

Satan wants as he continues to kill, steal, and destroy beneath our noses. Satan will do anything he can to blind the eyes of unbelievers.

Supernatural signs are not foundations for faith. Satan may come as an angel of light and perform miracles that we perceive as "good," such as physical healings or shows of supernatural power. Evil is often mingled with good making it difficult to spot. Satan deceives, copies, distorts, and distracts from the truth. This is also why discernment is required regarding miracles, the supernatural, or the spirit realm.

Jesus said in John 14:6 that no one comes to the Father except through Him. There are no other gods before Him. Any spirit or person who does not proclaim and submit to the Lordship of Jesus Christ aligns with the enemy. Therefore, we must stay rooted in Scripture and ask God daily for discernment. He will gently guide us on the path that leads to life.

Invitation to Journey Deeper:

- How aware of the spirit realm are you in daily life?
- What are examples of things the world calls good which are actually evil?

For Further Reading: John 10:10; 8:44 and 2 Corinthians 11:14

---

1. An outlook that stresses the potential value and goodness of human beings, attaching supreme importance to humanity rather than God.

BEING FOUND BY HIM

So if the Son sets you free from sin, then become a true son and be
unquestionably free!

—John 8:36, TPT

Jeremiah 29:13 promises, "You will seek Me and find Me when you
seek Me with all your heart." And when you find Him, you will know
Him. Knowing Him is what leads to becoming like Him.

God is after your heart. He promises to always be with you and never
leave you or forsake you. And though God is invisible, His Son is not.
He suffered as a man, died as a man, and was tempted, just like you and
me (though He never sinned).

When I was "lukewarm," I did not find Him because I was divided. I
was not seeking Jesus with my whole heart. Making Jesus the Lord of
my life changed everything. I was found by Him after 46 years of only
knowing *about* Him, and now I am being made like Him daily because
I know Him. The only thing standing in our way is the "self," which is
why we must be committed to the testimony of Jesus and uncommitted
to our own lives. In other words, we must become living sacrifices,
trusting in the will and the ways of the Father.

I believe that St. Francis wrote some of the most poignant words
describing what a living sacrifice looks like:

The Prayer of St. Francis

Lord, make me an instrument of your peace,
Where there is hatred, let me sow love;
where there is injury, pardon;
where there is doubt, faith;
where there is despair, hope;

where there is darkness, light;
where there is sadness, joy;

O Divine Master grant that I may not so much seek to be
consoled as to console;
to be understood as to understand;
to be loved as to love.
For it is in giving that we receive;
it is in pardoning that we are pardoned;
and it is in dying that we are born to eternal life.[1]

I prayed this prayer with Abbe every night before bed when she was little, along with Romans 12:21. Today, as I read these words, it reminds me of what a living sacrifice looks like. Jesus only did and said what He saw the Father doing and saying, a perfect model for how we should live. Seek Him, find Him. Find Him, know Him. Know Him, and become like Him, a living sacrifice, pure and holy, tried and true.

Invitation to Journey Deeper:

- What does it mean to be a living sacrifice?
- What strikes you most about *The Prayer of St. Francis*?

For Further Reading: John 3:30

---

1. "Make Me an Instrument of Peace, Saint Francis Prayer," *Catholic Online*, accessed November 23, 2021, https://www.catholic.org/prayers/prayer.php?p=134.

BECOMING LIKE JESUS

The Lord your God will circumcise your hearts and the hearts of your descendants, so that you may love Him with all your heart and with all your soul, and live.

—Deuteronomy 30:6

I did not know what it meant to love Jesus intimately for most of my life. As an engineer and someone who relies very heavily on logic, I could understand the basic biblical worldview and what it meant to be a Christian, but I found it challenging to comprehend how we could have a real relationship with an invisible God. I didn't understand how you could love someone you couldn't see.

However, over the last few years, I have come to understand this great mystery. The Lord has led me on a profound healing journey. One of the turning points came when I embraced *emotional* vulnerability. I have always struggled with being able to open my heart to others. But with God's help, I began to explore my emotions and share them with Him and with others. In the process, I experienced a new level of freedom, love for His Word, and encounters with Jesus!

This new freedom allowed me be to be fully myself which innately impacted my ability to connect with God. Slowly, I began to experience a genuine internal transformation. Jesus in me is taking up more and more space, and my relationship with others and with God will never be the same.

Jesus embodies the perfect expression of sacrificial, selfless, and unconditional *agape* love.[1] This is the love that heals us from the inside out. If we look to the person of Jesus, the physical manifestation of our invisible God, if we truly behold His character and His perfect love for us, how could we not fall in love with Him? The more we love Jesus intimately, the more we will naturally emulate Him and look like Him.

The love of God is changing me from the inside out and redefining my experience on earth as someone who has the mind of Christ and wants to please God and fulfil His plan. I see this transformation daily as I connect with those in great pain, those with intellectual, emotional, or physical disabilities, those who have recently accepted Jesus, and those ahead of me on the journey. God is using me to help others grow, and He is sending others to help *me* grow. We each have a vital role and purpose that manifests itself through *relationships*. This is one of the benefits of being a member of the family of God.

So today, I encourage you to open your heart to the intimate, *agape* love of Jesus. His love will breathe healing on you, your family, and your friendships. What's more, it will usher you into greater union with Christ, moulding you into His image. We not only get to know Jesus, we get to be His hands and feet on the earth and experience Him in others and in His glorious creation. Jesus is the source of all life! He is truth. He is the tree of life!

Invitation to Journey Deeper:

- When have you experienced *agape* love (in giving or receiving)?
- In what ways have you experienced healing through Jesus?
- Is there any area you desire healing today?
- What does it mean to be in union with Jesus?

For Further Reading: 1 Corinthians 6:17

---

1. *Agape* is the Greek word for "love" in the selfless sense; it is a choice and requires nothing in return. ("What does Agape really mean?" *Christianity Today*, accessed November 23, 2021, https://www.christianity.com/wiki/christian-terms/what-does-agape-love-really-mean-in-the-bible.html.)

SONS AND DAUGHTERS

The Spirit you received does not make you slaves, so that you live in fear again; rather, the Spirit you received brought about your adoption to sonship. And by Him we cry, "Abba, Father."

—Romans 8:15

Everyone starts out life on earth as a spiritual orphan. But through Jesus, we have the incredible privilege of being sons and daughters of God. As our Father, God is the source, provider, and foundation of our authority. He loves each and every one of us. Just think, we are now all children of God. You and I are family, brothers and sisters, one in the body of Christ.

"For in Him we live and move and have our being." As some of your own poets have said, "We are His offspring."

—Acts 17:28

As believers, we have free access to the Father and can confidently approach the throne of grace, just as any child can with a good and loving dad. Imagine, the Creator of the universe's greatest desire is that we enter into a relationship with Him as our Father!

And when we do, we no longer live as orphans. Instead, God chose to adopt us into His own family by drawing us near to Him. The Bible tells us He was not obligated in any way to do this. It wasn't just by chance or mistake; He wanted to do it... *and it gave Him great pleasure.*

That is ultimately who God is: He is our Father, and as Psalm 100:3 explains, "we are His people, the sheep of His pasture."

In the years I lived apart from God (for all the various reasons), I lived as an orphan. I did not find my identity in my Father in heaven. I found it in the things of this world. Knowing God helps us understand who we are. When I could have claimed sonship, I claimed money, success, my titles, abilities, and what others thought of me as my identity. All those things will ultimately fade away and are EXHAUSTING to maintain, but Kingdom treasure lasts forever.

The thing about this world is that it is fleeting. None of the things I put my hope in ever truly satisfied, not the way being embraced by the Father does. Even better? God doesn't change. Where the world is wavering and built on shifting sand, a life built on God is solid. He is our rock, our firm foundation. I now live my life as a son, and increasingly, what I do in life flows from the truth of my identity as a son first, living from God's unconditional love, approval, and acceptance through Christ. However, it has been quite a journey. Learning to live as a son is a growing process as we renew our minds. No matter where we are on the journey, we get to come to the Father as His children, safe and secure, resting and at peace in His goodness.

Invitation to Journey Deeper:

- Are you living as a son or daughter of God?
- How have you lived as an orphan? Are there ways you are still living independently from God?
- Who do you say you are? Who does God say you are? Take time to ask Him and write down what He says.

For Further Reading: Hebrews 4:16 and Ephesians 1:5

LEARN FROM THE BEST

Do not merely listen to the word, and so deceive yourselves. Do what it says. Anyone who listens to the word but does not do what it says is like someone who looks at his face in a mirror and, after looking at himself, goes away and immediately forgets what he looks like. But whoever looks intently into the perfect law that gives freedom, and continues in it—not forgetting what they have heard, but doing it— they will be blessed in what they do.

—James 1:22-25

The Bible is full of life wisdom and leadership lessons. In fact, John Maxwell, #1 New York Times bestselling author and world-renowned leadership expert, builds his entire leadership, mentoring, and coaching business based on biblical truths. When he and his team go into large companies, executives and staff will sometimes probe him where he got his cutting-edge material. He tells them they don't want to know. But if they press him, John reveals this "cutting edge material" is actually from the ancient teachings of the Bible.

In Scripture, the men and women, kings, queens, judges, military leaders, governors, prophets, teachers, and preachers all serve as examples of what to do and what not to do as leaders. Some began with promise and ended in disgrace. Others began with less than nothing and rose to great prominence, eventually leading their people to freedom and prosperity.

There is something to be learnt from each leader in the Bible. I personally have always been drawn to King David. A shepherd and musician who became a great warrior, and later, a beloved king, David was a man who experienced both great success and failure while managing to keep his heart after God. The Bible also reveals that David had immense struggles with lust, even resorting to murder to cover up his sin to get what he wanted. Eventually, he fully repented and turned his heart back to the Father. In fact, the Bible calls David a man after God's own heart... he had a New Covenant understanding of the gospel one thousand years before Christ.

Transformation flows, first from our hearts, then to our families, and then externally to things like our communities, businesses, etc. I believe that the life of a company runs parallel to the life of its leader. God can transform and sanctify a business, just like any man or woman. My heart's desire is to run a Kingdom business with *a heart after God*.

For me, that means I apply the biblical principles of excellence, creativity, and co-creating with God into the daily rhythms and functions of my company. Doing so removes the pressure to perform, compete, or behave in ways that are anti-God or based on human effort alone. With God at the helm, His peace prevails, and all glory belongs to Him.

Invitation to Journey Deeper:

- How is God a part of your daily life and decision-making?
- What part of your life (work, family, serving, relationships, etc.) can you invite God into in a new way?

For Further Reading: 1 Samuel 13:14

CHOSEN LEADERS

So Christ Himself gave the apostles, the prophets, the evangelists, the pastors and teachers, to equip His people for works of service, so that the body of Christ may be built up...

—Ephesians 4:11-12

The culture in my company has visibly changed since we started to apply biblical wisdom and standards to our behaviour. We are safer and kinder while being more honest, transparent, vulnerable, and direct. We have healthy boundaries and discipline over our time, habits, and communication. We've grown as a team and a family in trust and generosity towards one another. The fruit of these changes shows up in our interactions with each other, our customers, and our suppliers.

God is in the process of building His house, a Kingdom company reflecting His nature that glorifies Him. It is a Kingdom community where believers and non believers can thrive and enjoy the Kingdom. It is a house of prayer, a church, and a business all in one. In short, we are creating a place where God is honored and glorified.

How has this transformation taken place?

We have invited God into every aspect of His company. I say *His company* as I am only a steward of what God has given to me. Many know that our company belongs to God, and we have created space for people to meet with Him anytime, both physically and spiritually. Our work is an act of worship as it is unto the Lord. We have a prayer room available at all times, and we are learning to seek God's wisdom and understanding in every decision, at every level. Our senior leadership team prays together each morning and takes communion together on occasion. God takes precedence in all things. We also have prophetic intercessors who pray for the employees and the business as a whole.

The primary fruit and success? Transformed hearts! Transformed people transform their families, workplace, friendships, and beyond.

Biblical wisdom asks believers to run their businesses as their ministry because God sees and values all our work, whether "full-time ministry" or "business," the same. To Him, it's all ministry and what matters most is our love for Him and others.

Whether your position is at a church, in a classroom, at the dinner table with your family or at the CEO desk on the top floor of a high-rise, God sees each of us as ministers of His gospel. We are all walking side by side as equal partners in the greater church leadership. God works through whomever He chooses to be a leader, and the way to be a godly leader begins with relationship and is developed though a love and understanding of His Word.

Invitation to Journey Deeper:

- How does the Bible and its wisdom play a part in your life?
- In what areas of your life are you a leader? Is God calling you to lead in a new way?
- If your life is a business and you are its leader, are you running a Kingdom business?

For Further Reading: 1 Corinthians 10:31

BELIEVING IN THE WORD

Your word is a lamp for my feet, a light on my path.

—*Psalm 119:105*

The Bible is a collection of books. It was written over fifteen hundred years by dozens of authors inspired by the Holy Spirit. The Bible is the inerrant, inspired, beautiful, and profound Word of God. As the Bible says of itself in 2 Timothy 3:16-17, "All Scripture is God-breathed and is useful for teaching, rebuking, correcting and training in right-eousness, so that the servant of God may be thoroughly equipped for every good work." The Bible is our guide, showing us how to live. It instructs us about God and His plan, pointing us towards Christ. It is also a place of relationship and encountering God.

The spiritual armour Paul speaks of in Ephesians 6:17 encourages us to "Take the helmet of salvation and the sword of the Spirit, which is the word of God." Interestingly, this is the only offensive weapon Paul mentions. Like Jesus, we can respond to the enemy's attacks by reciting the truth as found in Scripture. Believers must immerse themselves in the Word of God.

> "There are four principles we need to maintain: First, read the Word
> of God. Second, consume the Word of God until it consumes you.
> Third, believe the Word of God. Fourth, act on the Word of God."
>
> —Smith Wigglesworth[1]

For a new believer, I recommend starting your Bible journey with the New Testament. Begin with the Gospel of John and then move on to Matthew, Mark, and Luke. My personal favourite translation is *The Passion Translation* by Brian Simmons. This version has brought Scrip-ture to life in a beautiful new way for me. The YouVersion Bible App is a free app that allows you to read or listen to the Bible in various translations. The app also offers countless devotionals, videos, and reading plans to keep you on track with your daily Bible study.

I challenge you to memorise as much Scripture as you can. Why? Because God encourages us to do so in Colossians 3:16 for the purpose of teaching and admonishing others (and ourselves). It increases our faith and produces hope.

> *Let the message of Christ dwell among you richly as you teach and admonish one another with all wisdom through psalms, hymns, and songs from the Spirit, singing to God with gratitude in your hearts.*
>
> —Colossians 3:16

Memorising Scripture gives us wisdom and warns us against sin. It helps us recognise any lies or doctrinal errors we may have encountered and points us back towards the truth. His Word is the lamp that lights our path! We can believe in God. We can believe in His Son and the gift of salvation. And we can believe in the promises contained in His Word!

Invitation to Journey Deeper:

The Bible is filled with so many incredible testimonies which we can learn from and claim for our own lives. What God did in the past, He will do it again as He is the same yesterday, today, and forever! Consider starting your Scripture memory journey with the following list. It may take you some time to plant these deep in your heart and be able to recall them from memory, but it will be worth it!

- Matthew 6:33
- Psalm 37:4
- Romans 8:28-30
- Philippians 4:13

- Isaiah 54:17
- Zechariah 4:6
- 2 Corinthians 12:9
- James 1:2-5
- Hebrews 11:1
- 3 John 2:11
- Romans 8:1
- Jeremiah 29:11
- Numbers 6:24-26
- Galatians 5:22-23
- Psalm 139:1-3

For Further Reading: Psalm 119:104

---

1. "Smith Wigglesworth," *Quote Fancy*, accessed November 23, 2021, https://quote
fancy.com/quote/908268/Smith-Wigglesworth-There-are-four-principles-we-need-
to-maintain-First-read-the-Word-of.

Part Two

Experiencing God

Jesus came so there would be no separation between God and mankind, for now, and all of eternity. He restored us to a full relationship! Knowing God and growing in His likeness requires spending time with Him. Doing so renews our minds to the truth of our life in union with Him. Just as with any relationship, the more attention we give to Christ, the more we learn to be in tune with the Spirit and His leading.

Hearing God's voice is not always easy. Sometimes it may come through an audible voice as it did for Moses, and other times it may come as a quiet whisper the way Elijah experienced His leading. God has even made Himself known through a donkey, angels, the outpouring of the Holy Spirit, through visions, dreams, and by speaking in tongues and the interpretation of tongues. God is always speaking; we only need to take the time to listen.

What an incredible thing: God speaks directly to us! And we have the privilege of entering into conversation with Him. Our God is always accessible. In fact, *He wants to spend time with us.* By being in relationship with the Father, we get to experience the love that He offers. In return, we become more like Him, freely giving the love we have received to those who need it most.

The biggest challenge is letting go. For me, this looked like getting out of my head and into my heart (where the Kingdom of God resides, the home of our indwelling God). My natural tendency is to want to understand how everything works, but the mysteries of God are to be experienced, not always understood.

Your primary purpose is to know God and to worship Him. The more you know Him, the more you will experience His love. As a result, our love for Him (and others) will grow. In this section, I will share the basic concepts required to move into the fullness of a relationship with God. These are things I wish I knew much earlier in life. With that in mind, I invite you to join me in learning to experience God and giving Him room to meet you wherever you are on your journey.

PRAYER

Do not be anxious about anything, but in every situation, by prayer and petition, with thanksgiving, present your requests to God.

—*Philippians 4:6*

God limited Himself to work in partnership with people. Prayer is simply having a conversation with God, giving Him permission to work on the earth. Before I entered into a deep, committed relationship with God, I refused to pray aloud, especially in front of people. As a result, my prayer life was shallow, and I even *paid* other people to pray for my business on my behalf. Today, my personal prayer life is totally transformed (though I still covet the prayers of others).

When we pray, we become more aligned with God and His purposes. His desires become our desires. Graham Cooke, an author and speaker specialising in corporate and individual Christian development, explains, "Prayer, in its simplest form, is finding out what God wants to do and then asking Him to do it."[1]

The answers to our prayers may not look like we expect, so we must trust God, His goodness, and His ways. The more we know Him, the more we will become like Him, and the more we will pray like Him. But no matter what, we can rest assured knowing God's ways are higher than our ways, and He has a plan to make all things new.

For I know the plans I have for you," declares the Lord, "plans to prosper you and not to harm you, plans to give you hope and a future."

—*Jeremiah 29:11*

The thing is, God *wants* to talk to us. Sure, God could do anything He wants without us, but He designed things to work in and through us. How? One way is prayer.

God is almighty and all-powerful, but He is also relational and longs for us to come to Him and tell Him what we need. He desires time with us. He wants to enjoy His creation (us). He delights in spending time with us to teach us what we need to know. He wants to laugh with us and celebrate together. And He promises to comfort us when we are in pain. God says in Jeremiah 33:3, "Call to Me and I will answer you..." Prayer is the key to accomplishing any purpose. God answers our prayers when they align with heaven and His will. No prayer is too big or too small for God to answer. He cares about the small, seemingly insignificant moments of our days, and He is big enough to move in the most challenging areas of our lives.

As children of God, it is only natural to spend time with our heavenly Father. We do so through prayer. He is available to us all the time and wants us at our best and at our worst. While the answers to our prayers may not always be what we expected, God know best and we can depend on Him to always answer.

Invitation to Journey Deeper:

- Does God want to spend more time with you in this season?
- God created us for a relationship with Him. Imagine if your child, parent, spouse, or good friend stopped speaking to you. How would that feel? Consider what God might feel like when you don't spend time with Him.
- If you are unsure how to begin praying, consider the following acronym as a simple reminder: **P**raise, **R**epent, **A**sk, and **Y**ield.

For Further Reading: Isaiah 55:8-9; 43:19

---

1. Graham Cooke, "Crafted Prayer: The Joy of Always Getting Your Prayers Answered," *Goodreads*, accessed December 30, 2021, https://www.goodreads.com/quotes/848127-prayer-in-it-s-simplest-form-is-finding-out-what-god.

HOW SHOULD WE PRAY

Our Beloved Father, dwelling in the heavenly realms, may the glory of Your name be the center on which our lives turn. Manifest Your Kingdom realm, and cause Your every purpose to be fulfilled on earth, just as it is in heaven. We acknowledge You as our Provider of all we need each day. Forgive us the wrongs we have done as we ourselves release forgiveness to those who have wronged us. Rescue us every time we face tribulation and set us free from evil. For You are the King who rules with power and glory forever. Amen.

—Matthew 6:9-13, TPT

God gives us clear instructions for how to pray throughout Scripture. God gave us the Lord's Prayer (above) as a specific example of how to pray. Jesus shared this prayer with His disciples, which served as a roadmap for the early church, who had great reverence for it. Sadly, many today consider it a "common" prayer, missing its incredible power and significance. (There are many wonderful books written on the Lord's Prayer and its remarkable spiritual depth.)

The Lord's Prayer outlines how God calls us to pray *daily*. It begins by acknowledging that God is our Father and affirms His lordship. From there, it guides us to align ourselves with God's purposes *on earth as it is in heaven*. It encourages us to thank God for His provision and to step into the forgiveness Jesus offers us and then offer it to others. Finally, it tells us to call on Him to rescue us and deliver us from the enemy. The prayer covers every base, from who God is (our Father) to who we are (His children). It explains how to partner with Him and how we can trust God to provide for us and to protect us. It also clarifies how we should treat others. The following verse also gives the keys to positioning ourselves for prayer.

117

If My people, who are called by My name, will humble themselves and
pray and seek My face and turn from their wicked ways, then I will
hear from heaven, and I will forgive their sin and will heal their land.

—2 *Chronicles* 7:14

Humility opens our ears to hear from the Lord. Jesus says in John 10:27, "My sheep listen to My voice; I know them, and they follow me." To hear, we must be quiet. When we pray what God says to us, we become like Jesus.

One place to start your prayer journey is in Scripture. Pray the Word. Begin in the Psalms. Turn your thoughts to Jesus and read your selected verses out loud. You can also pray simple prayers, like "Help me, Jesus." (This one is always very effective!) Or a favourite of John Wimber, "Come Holy Spirit."[1] When we call on the Lord, He is faithful to answer.

Invitation to Journey Deeper:

- Set aside time to quiet your heart and mind and listen for God's voice. What do you hear?
- Find a passage of Psalms and read it aloud as you align with God in prayer.

For Further Reading: 1 Samuel 3:10

---

1. John Wimber was a global influencer and leader of the Vineyard church movement before his death in 1997.

DESIGNED TO WORSHIP

Rejoice always, pray continually, give thanks in all circumstances; for this is God's will for you in Christ Jesus.

—1 Thessalonians 5:16-18

Prayer and faith are intrinsically connected. God instructs us to call things that are not yet manifest as though they were. This is praying in faith and expectation.

Faith is reaching into the supernatural to bring it into the natural. *The Passion Translation* declares in Hebrews 11:1, "Now faith brings our hopes into reality and becomes the foundation needed to acquire the things we long for. It is all the evidence required to prove what is still unseen." Through faith, we declare His Word and the things God has spoken over our lives, marriages, children, families, finances, friends, cities, nations, etc. One powerful example that I use is to speak "I am" declarations in accordance with the Word of God:

- Through Christ, I am made perfect. (Hebrews 10:14)
- I am a new creation; the old is gone, the new has come! (2 Corinthians 5:17)
- I am the righteousness of God. (2 Corinthians 5:21)

Like prayer and faith, prayer and worship are inseparable. I used to think that worship was only about singing at the beginning of a church service, but it is meant to be our Kingdom lifestyle. To worship God is to adore and delight in Him, making Him the centre of our lives and expressing our love to Him. Worship is valuing God above everything. Worship is about connection and connection is about relationship. Even our work, when done unto the Lord, becomes worship. (Note: in Hebrew, the word *abad* references both "work" and "worship." They are inherently linked!)[1]

Our Creator designed us to worship Him. Doing so brings life, hope, peace, and joy. We can worship by singing, preaching, praying, giving, pondering Him, resting in His presence, and thanking Him. Our whole life can and should be a continual act of worship as worship is all about God's presence and creating the space for Him to manifest. In the words of William Temple, Archbishop of Canterbury, "Worship is the submission of all of our nature to God... the surrender of will to His purpose... "[2]

Praise releases God's power! Praise heals! Praise fills and transforms! As author, evangelist, and founder of Harvest Evangelism and Transform Our World Network, Ed Silvoso says, "Labor is the premier expression of worship on Earth, and every believer is a minister."[3] When done unto the Lord, our daily work becomes an act of worship. It doesn't matter what your job is, from a mother to an astronaut, a janitor to a teacher, or an artist to a pastor. God designed us to partner with Him in all that we do.

Invitation to Journey Deeper:

- How are you using your life to worship God? How does your perspective on work change considering its link to worship?
- What part of your life have you left God out of (intentionally or unintentionally)? How can you include Him in it?

For Further Reading: Romans 4:17

---

1. Dr. Annechiena Sneller-Vrolijk, "Biblical Vocabulary: עבד ("To Serve")," *Biblword*, accessed December 30, 2021, https://www.biblword.net/biblical-vocabulary-serving-the-lord/.
2. Sus Schmitt, "'The Purifying of Imagination' – William Temple," *God Fully Known*, accessed December 30, 2021, https://godfullyknown.blog/2021/02/02/the-purifying-of-imagination-william-temple/.
3. Ed Silvoso, *Transformation: Change The Marketplace and You Change the World* (Ventura: Regal Books, 2007), 29.

I AM

DECLARATIONS

—————

God desires for you to see yourself through His eyes, made in His image. As you spend time in prayer, read the following "I am" declarations aloud. Claim your true identity as a new creation, designed with purpose, for His purposes. The enemy no longer has a grip on you!

- I am a child of God. I am a saint. I am a new creation in Christ, old things have passed away, and all things have become new. *2 Corinthians 5:17*

- I am born again and born of God. *John 1:13; 3:3*

- I am in Christ. I am a citizen of heaven. *Philippians 3:20*

- I am a friend of Christ. *John 15:15*

- I am a temple, a dwelling place of God. His Spirit and His life dwell within me. *1 Corinthians 6:19*

- I am the righteousness of God in Christ. *2 Corinthians 5:21*

- I am holy through Jesus' sacrifice. *Hebrews 10:10*

- I am an expression of Christ. I am a child of light. *John 12:36*

- I am seated with Christ in heavenly places. *Ephesians 2:6*

- I am a recipient of every spiritual blessing in the heavenly places in Christ. *Ephesians 1:3*

- I am a child of God and will resemble Christ when He returns. *John 1:12*

- I am a son of light, not of darkness. I am chosen by God, holy and dearly loved. *1 Thessalonians 5:5*

- I am free forever from condemnation. *Romans 8:1*

- I am crucified with Christ, and it is no longer I who live but Christ who lives in me. *Galatians 2:20*

- I have the spirit of power, love, and self-discipline. *2 Timothy 1:7*

- I grow in the grace and knowledge of our Lord and Saviour Jesus Christ. *2 Peter 3:18*

DAILY
PRAYERS

"Is anyone among you in trouble? Let them pray. Is anyone happy? Let them sing songs of praise." — *JAMES 5:13*

Scripture calls us to pray daily, not worrying about tomorrow, for tomorrow will worry for itself. There was a time when my prayer life was almost non-existent. I spent little time with God, and as a result, my lifestyle reflected my desires instead of His. Now, I love to pray! Each day as I spend more time in God's presence, I learn to hear His voice more clearly. His words guide me and shape me to be more like Him. I can't imagine my life without His guidance!

There are many ways to pray and many things and people to pray for. For me, I like to start the day in the Spirit, inviting God into my steps from the moment I wake up: "Good morning Jesus, good morning Holy Spirit, good morning Father, this is your beloved son/daughter _____ !" Then I ask God to speak into my life and reveal His heart to me as I surrender everything to Him. This helps me know who and what to pray for and receive direction (or correction) from the Lord.

The following page provides you with a few sample prayers I might pray to start my day, but keep in mind that your relationship with the Father will be unique to you. I encourage you to spend time in His presence, getting to know His voice because the more you do, the more you will learn His heart and be formed in His likeness. I can assure you, it will be worth your time!

A PRAYER TO START MY DAY

Jesus, I ask for Your glorious freedom. I ask for grace for this day and dedicate myself to You in body, soul, and spirit. I ask for the Spirit of wisdom and revelation in the knowledge of Christ. I give You my heart and ask for intimacy with You. Open the eyes of my heart. I declare that my heart is completely Yours. I surrender all to You and declare — may Your will be done, not mine. May Your Holy Spirit fill me to overflow and guide me in all my ways. Help me to be a lover of truth and a passionate worshiper. Lord, fill me with Your desires for me. In Jesus' name, I pray. Amen!

DECLARATIONS I MAY SPEAK OVER MY LIFE

I am created for blessing and decree His blessing around my life and all that pertains to me. I am strong in the Lord and His strength. I put on the full armour of God. I declare no weapon formed against my family or me will prosper. I can do all things through Christ who strengthens me. Greater is He who is in me than He who is in this world. I rest in the peace, protection, and strength of my almighty God. I walk in great peace in my spirit as I know God's great favour is upon me, preparing each moment of this day, opening doors before me, and removing obstacles.

Great grace abundantly blesses me, fills me, and empowers me each and every day. I declare Jesus is the Lord of my life! To God enthroned and to our Lord Jesus Christ, be all praise and honour and glory and dominion forever and ever. I declare all the kingdoms of this world will submit to the kingdom of our God. Your kingdom come, Your will be done on earth as it is in heaven. Lord, do eternal things through me in my life.

PRAYING LIKE

THE EPHESIANS

When you pray Scripture, it fills you with revelation and the love of God while aligning you with His Word. The book of Ephesians includes two powerful prayers for you to declare over yourself and others, both believers and nonbelievers.

PRAYER 1

My heart is always full and overflowing with thanks to God for you as I constantly remember you in my prayers. I pray that the Father of glory, the God of our Lord Jesus Christ, would impart to you the riches of the Spirit of wisdom and the Spirit of revelation to know Him through your deepening intimacy with Him. I pray that the light of God will illuminate the eyes of your imagination, flooding you with light, until you experience the full revelation of the hope of His calling — that is, the wealth of God's glorious inheritances that He finds in us, His holy ones! I pray that you will continually experience the immeasurable greatness of God's power made available to you through faith. Then your lives will be an advertisement of this immense power as it works through you! This is the mighty power that was released when God raised Christ from the dead and exalted Him to the place of highest honor and supreme authority in the heavenly realm!

—Ephesians 1:16-20, TPT

PRAYER 2

So I kneel humbly in awe before the Father of our Lord Jesus, the Messiah, the perfect Father of every father and child in heaven and on the earth. And I pray that He would unveil within you the unlimited riches of His glory and favor until supernatural strength floods your innermost being with His divine might and explosive power. Then, by constantly using your faith, the life of Christ will be released deep inside you, and the resting place of His love will become the very source and root of your life. Then you will be empowered to discover what every holy one experiences — the great magnitude of the astonishing love of Christ in all its dimensions. How deeply intimate and far-reaching is His love! How enduring and inclusive it is! Endless love beyond measurement that transcends our understanding — this extravagant love pours into you until you are filled to overflowing with the fullness of God!

—Ephesians 3:14-19, TPT

As you declare these words, expect God to reveal Himself to you and bless you in the fullness of His Spirit. For, as Psalm 16:11 declares, "You make known to me the path of life; You will fill me with joy in Your presence, with eternal pleasures at Your right hand."

A PRAYER FOR

NONBELIEVERS

As Christians, praying for those who don't know the Lord is a critical part of our faith journey. Consider the following prayer as an example of how to pray for nonbelievers. Fill the person's name in the spaces provided.

Lord, Your will is that none shall perish and that all come to repentance. I come into agreement with Your will and ask for Your mercy on _____ .

Jesus, I know the only way people come to You is by the Father who sent You. I ask that You would make _____ desperate for Your love. Will You draw _____'s heart to Jesus, that (he/she) will know You and spend eternity with You? I ask that _____ be given the opportunity to make Jesus Lord.

Lord, will You remove the veil from _____'s heart and eyes? I ask for You to move upon his/her heart to accept the truth of Christ and turn to You. I pray that the light of God will illuminate the eyes of _____'s imagination, flooding (him/her) with light until (he/she) experiences the full revelation of the hope of His calling. I pray the life of Christ will be released deep inside of _____ , and the resting place of His love will become the very source and root of _____'s life. Lord, I ask for You to give a new heart and a new spirit. Replace (his/her) heart of stone and give (him/her) a heart of flesh. Give him/her a heart to know You as Your people and to know You as (his/her) God. Lord, empower _____ with the revelation of Your love for (him/her). Open _____ 's eyes to (his/her) true condition, so that (he/she) may turn from darkness to the light and from the power of Satan to the power of God.

Lord, I acknowledge that only You can change hearts, and I believe that You will do it for _____ . I speak peace and blessing over _____ in the mighty name of Jesus! I speak of the things that are not as though they are and thank You for _____'s salvation! It is finished!

Lord, thank You for Your love, grace, and mercy over _____'s life. I pray this in the mighty name of Jesus. Hallelujah! Amen!

Praying for nonbelievers is our responsibility and privilege as followers of Christ.

GOD SPEAKS

I no longer call you servants, because a servant does not know his master's business. Instead, I have called you friends, for everything that I learned from My Father I have made known to you.

—John 15:15

Every person can hear God's voice, but we often don't recognise it. Learning to listen to our heavenly Father is one of the highest callings of Christians. His voice transforms our lives and develops our character. Our relationship with God is life's greatest treasure, and developing an ear that is sensitive to His voice is critical to developing that relationship. He created us for relationship!

What sort of genuine relationship involves only one party talking? None!

Real, meaningful relationships develop from a two-way dialogue. That means we need to learn to listen to God as much as we need to practice speaking to Him. Mark Virkler, founder of Communion with God Ministries and author of over 50 books, absolutely nails it with this short but powerful definition:

> "When I learned to recognize the voice of God as the bubbling flow
> of spontaneous ideas that welled up from my heart as I fixed my eyes
> on Jesus, I discovered a new way of living..."
>
> —Mark Virkler[1]

For decades, I thought hearing from God was a privilege reserved for prophets and a select few men and women. I had no idea that communicating with God was something available to everyone. Jesus teaches in John 10:27, "My sheep listen to My voice; I know them, and they follow Me."

God communicates to us in many forms. He communicates through the Bible. He also speaks through other people, circumstances, signs, promptings, numbers, wonders, miracles, angels, visions, dreams, nature, and occasionally, He might even speak through a donkey, as He did to the prophet Balaam.

However, hearing from God is not always so dramatic. He also speaks through our senses, perception, feelings (intuition), and deep inner-knowing. All these forms of communication come together to more fully experience God speaking to us!

> The Lord said, "Go out and stand on the mountain in the presence of the Lord, for the Lord is about to pass by." Then a great and powerful wind tore the mountains apart and shattered the rocks before the Lord, but the Lord was not in the wind. After the wind there was an earthquake, but the Lord was not in the earthquake. After the earthquake came a fire, but the Lord was not in the fire. And after the fire came a gentle whisper. When Elijah heard it, he pulled his cloak over his face and went out and stood at the mouth of the cave. Then a voice said to him, "What are you doing here, Elijah?"
>
> —1 Kings 19:11-13

When I quiet myself before the Lord, I can often hear His still, small voice (although not usually audibly).

Journaling and processing situations through the lens of God's Word and truth helps me recognise how He is leading me. Because we sit in heavenly places with Christ, we can see situations from His perspective. Earthly perspectives no longer bind us. We can settle into the truth of His ultimate victory and act accordingly.

Invitation to Journey Deeper:

- Have you ever heard God's voice? What did it sound like? What did He say to you?
- Is it easy or difficult for you to hear God's voice? Do you feel like He hears you?
- How can you practice listening? Is there someone you can share this journey with to help you discern His voice?

For Further Reading: Numbers 22:28 and Ephesians 2:6

---

1. Mark and Patti Virkler, *4 Keys to Hearing God's Voice* (Shippensburg: Destiny Image Publishers, INC., 2010), 23.

A HEAVENLY LANGUAGE

Suddenly a sound like the blowing of a violent wind came from heaven and filled the whole house where they were sitting. They saw what seemed to be tongues of fire that separated and came to rest on each of them. All of them were filled with the Holy Spirit and began to speak in other tongues as the Spirit enabled them.

—Acts 2:2-4

Speaking in tongues is a spiritual gift meant to edify and strengthen both us and others that can only be received after being baptized in the Holy Spirit. Baptism in the Holy Spirit and the speaking of tongues is not the same as the salvation experience. Those who are saved can love Jesus and have a vibrant relationship with Him, but those who are baptized in the Holy Spirit and receive the gift of tongues receive a passion for Jesus and supernatural power in a way others do not. The baptism of the Holy Spirit is so important that Jesus told early believers in Luke 24:49 to "...stay in the city until you have been clothed with power from on high." Empowered by the Holy Spirit, believers speak and pray the exact will of God through the gift of tongues, even though they may not understand what they are saying.

...and asked them, "Did you receive the Holy Spirit when you believed?" They answered, "No, we have not even heard that there is a Holy Spirit."

—Acts 19:2

Not all receive the gift of tongues, but it is promised for all. To move in signs and wonders as a believer, you must receive the gift of the Holy Spirit, daily receiving a fresh baptism and growing in the spirit. Receiving your prayer language is an important step in walking out the greater things.

In Acts 2, the Holy Spirit descended on a group of about 120 believers on the day of Pentecost.[1] The result was the first recorded instance of speaking in tongues (glossolalia). According to pastor and author Dr. Sam Storms, "The Holy Spirit personally crafts or creates a special and unique language that enables a Christian to speak to God in prayer, praise, and thanksgiving."[2]

Tongues serve as a sign and a wonder to unbelievers, although the demonic also has counterfeit tongues. This is why the gift of interpretation of tongues is necessary for corporate worship gatherings for the sake of those listening. Praying in tongues privately can produce great spiritual fruit when used alongside prayer and praise.

There was a season of 90 days where my believing community spoke in tongues daily (throughout the day) and experienced increased faith and fruit of the Spirit as a result. In the words of the apostle Paul in 1 Corinthians 14:15, "So what shall I do? I will pray with my spirit, but I will also pray with my understanding; I will sing with my spirit, but I will also sing with my understanding." Scripture is clear that we may not all receive this gift, but we can certainly all benefit from it.

Early on in this book's production, I met a young man in a coffee shop. We struck up a conversation and spoke for three hours about life, God, and the transformative power of the Holy Spirit. He confided in me that he had an ongoing pornography addiction that was contributing to a great deal of personal shame and pain in his marriage. He greatly desired more of God and to live out of a new level of purity. As I left, I gave him the copy of the book I was working on (printed out on a very large stack of computer paper) and my email address.

A few weeks went by. The young man wrote me and said that he had been faithfully reading the book and when he read this reflection, he decided he needed to be filled with the Holy Spirit. Not only was he filled with the Holy Spirit that day, but he has been experiencing healing and deliverance in many areas of his life since. His family and I are still in touch and I am amazed at how the Holy Spirit is daily transforming this young man into the image of Christ.

Remember: God calls us to pray without ceasing. The use of tongues activates our spirit's leading to a more powerful prayer life for both us and others.

Invitation to Journey Deeper:

- Have you prayed to receive the baptism of the Holy Spirit? Why or why not?
- If you have received the gift of tongues, are you using it to edify and strengthen yourself and the body of Christ?
- If you have not received the gift of tongues, what other gifts have you received from the Spirit, and how are you using them to edify the Lord?

For Further Reading: 1 Corinthians 12:1-11 and 1 Corinthians 14:4-5

---

1. Paul notes in Acts 1:15 that he "stood up among" about 120 believers at this time.
2. Sam Storms, "10 Things to Know about Speaking in Tongues," Crosswalk, accessed December 30, 2021, https://www.crosswalk.com/faith/spiritual-life/10-things-to-know-about-speaking-in-tongues.html.

SPIRIT-LED AND EMPOWERED

After they prayed, the place where they were meeting was shaken. And they were all filled with the Holy Spirit and spoke the word of God boldly.

—*Acts 4:31*

Speaking in tongues is a gift from the Father intended to bless both us and others. Brain scans show that there is a marked decrease in frontal lobe activity when someone is speaking in tongues. In other words, there is a noticeable decrease in self-control. Andrew Newberg, a scientist at the University of Pennsylvania, conducted a study on speaking in tongues and discovered some incredible findings:

> "'The part of the brain that normally makes them feel in control has been essentially shut down.' Another notable change was increased activity in the parietal region—the part of the brain that 'takes sensory information and tries to create a sense of self and how you relate to the rest of the world.' The findings make sense, says Newberg, because speaking in tongues involves relinquishing control while gaining a 'very intense experience of how the self relates to God.'"[1]

Newberg's study also showed that speaking in tongues results in a completely opposite response than those practicing meditation, which resulted in increased frontal lobe activity (i.e., more focus versus less focus).[2] What a wonderful example of how speaking in tongues is a truly Spirit-led physical experience.

Now, looking back at the church in Acts, their building was shaken when the Holy Spirit came upon them. Not only that, but they continued to speak the Word of God with boldness. The gift of tongues is in no way passive or without purpose. It came in with a thunderous roar that literally shook the building and empowered them to proclaim the name of Jesus with authority.

What if this happened in the church today? God is alive and active, eager to give good gifts as we are willing to receive them. The world is in desperate need of truth. Jesus explains how to spread this truth in Matthew 28:19: "Therefore go and make disciples of all nations, baptizing them in the name of the Father and of the Son and of the Holy Spirit." Like a father who gives his daughter a new bike for her birthday or sends his son off to school with a new pair of shoes, the Father delights when we use His gifts for His purposes!

Invitation to Journey Deeper:

If you are eager to receive the gift of tongues, I encourage you to follow the steps listed below. We are all encouraged to model our lives after Paul, just as he followed Christ's example.

- Humbly ask the Lord for the gift of tongues. (If you haven't yet received the Baptism of the Holy Spirit, this is the first step.)
- Open your mouth and let the words flow. You do not need to overthink or work for it.

For Further Reading: Acts 4:31 and 1 Corinthians 11:1

---

1. Constance Holden, "Tongues on the Mind: Psychiatrists Probe What Happens in the Brain When People 'Speak in Tongues,'" *Science*, accessed February 19, 2022, https://www.sciencemag.org/news/2006/11/tongues-mind.
2. Ibid.

LET GO

Humble yourselves before the Lord, and He will lift you up.

—James 4:10

Even when we have committed our whole lives to God, it can be challenging to let go of the pieces of our identity that we think make us who we are. They might not be bad things either. God has undoubtedly used my engineering brain for good. And yet, at times, it has gotten in the way of my walk with God.

I did not grow up in a home where speaking in tongues was a part of life. In fact, speaking in tongues did not become a part of my life until much later in my Christian walk after I was baptized in the Holy Spirit. For me, the idea of speaking in tongues sounded foolish, but God uses foolish things to confound the wise. As I grew in my faith and began to experience the deeper things of God, I reached a point where I was able to let myself go.

> "Great faith doesn't come out of great effort, but out of great surrender."
>
> —Bill Johnson[1]

At a leadership summit called Leadership Edge, one of the speakers asked who could not speak in tongues... I raised my hand. Everyone around me started praying over me as I surrendered whatever control I was holding onto and allowed the words and sounds of my heavenly language to come out of my mouth.

It didn't sound like much at first, but the more I let go, the more words poured out. I'll admit, it felt very awkward at first. It takes a measure of freedom to surrender our mind and body to move with the Holy Spirit.

Until that point in my life, I had prayed to receive tongues many times. However, to see a breakthrough, I had to let the engineering part of my brain go (the part of me which seeks to understand and apply reason). When I did, I experienced a different level of freedom and a new aspect of God. Letting go allowed God to lift me up.

Invitation to Journey Deeper:

- What are you holding onto that keeps you from experiencing the fullness of what God has to offer?
- Why is it difficult to let go of control and trust God will take the reins?

For Further Reading: 1 Corinthians 1:27

---

1. Bill Johnson, "All Bill Johnson Quotes About 'Surrender,'" *Inspiringquotes.us*, accessed February 19, 2022. https://www.inspiringquotes.us/author/1588-bill-john son/about-surrender.

A SINCERE HEART

He says, "Be still, and know that I am God; I will be exalted among the nations, I will be exalted in the earth."

—Psalm 46:10

The posture of our heart prepares us to hear God's voice more clearly. As you prepare to hear the voice of God, reflect on your motives. Are you truly ready to hear what God has to say? Is there possibly a selfish motive at the core of your desire to hear Him, or are you seeking to grow closer to Him and obey His voice and leading? Whose will do you seek?

Hearing from God is important, but our main focus must be a relationship with our heavenly Father. God wants us to spend time with Him. He wants to love us, and we get to love Him. Practically speaking, I begin by preparing my heart to spend time with God by praying the following prayer by Mark Virkler.

> *Lord, I draw near with a sincere heart, repentant and washed by the blood of my Lord and Saviour, Jesus Christ. I set aside my thoughts, my reasoning, my theology, my fears and my pride. I relax, cease my own strivings, and tune to Your flow within. Holy Spirit, I open my heart and mind to You. I ask that You anoint the eyes of my heart and enlighten my understanding. I ask that You grant me God's thoughts, God's pictures, God's emotions and God's creativity. Thank You for what You reveal.*
>
> *In Jesus' name, Amen*[1]

I will never forget when Bryn expressed her excitement at realising God not only wanted to speak with her but did speak to her during her first week at Youth With A Mission (YWAM) in Hawaii. The subject for the first week of discipleship training, for good reason, was hearing the voice of God! Something remarkable happens when you experience the relational, conversational aspect of hearing God.

Positioning ourselves to hear from God means removing all distractions, going into a quiet place, humbling ourselves before the Lord, and patiently and expectantly waiting on Him to move. Psalm 46:10 says, "Be still and know that I am God." This doesn't mean He can't or won't speak to us during a busy day or a loud meeting. However, discerning His voice in those spaces can be more challenging, especially at first.

After only a few years, I now hear Him more easily as His voice flows through the words I speak, my thoughts, my prayers, and my actions. Never forget, the Kingdom of heaven is within. We are temples of the Holy Spirit. It is not for us to force or coax God to speak. Rather, the act of positioning ourselves to receive from Him allows us to be attentive to His still small voice, whether it be in the quiet minutes before we start our day or the most stressful moments or seasons of our lives.

Invitation to Journey Deeper:

- Are you aware of any wrong motives when you pray? Check your heart and ask the Lord for forgiveness if there are any.
- Take a moment of silence to quiet your heart and mind. Read a few scriptures aloud or pray Mark's prayer as I often do. Practice letting go and wait to hear God's voice. What do you hear?

For Further Reading: 1 Corinthians 6:19

---

1. "Hear God Through Your Dreams Sample Lesson Two," *Christian Leadership for U: School of the Spirit*, accessed December 30, 2021, https://www.cluschoolofthespirit.com/lessons/hear-god-through-your-dreams-sample-lesson-two/.

WHOSE WORD?

And a voice came from heaven: "You are my Son, whom I love; with you I am well pleased."

—Mark 1:11

My first real understanding of how to hear God came from reading Mark and Patti Virkler's *4 Keys to Hearing God's Voice*. The Virklers explain the four keys as follows:

1. Stillness: Quiet yourself so you can hear God's voice.
2. Vision: Look for vision(s) as you pray.
3. Spontaneity: Recognise God's voice as spontaneous thoughts that light up in your mind.
4. Journaling: Write down the flow of thoughts and pictures.[1]

Thoughts from God are encouraging, truthful, filled with light, and edifying. These thoughts encourage, teach, and produce faith and hope. If your thoughts do not fit this description, you can safely conclude they are not from God. The enemy knows how to wound you. His words are not always obvious; they can even come through the voices of those we love the most. If a thought is not from God, it is either one of our own thoughts or from the enemy. Any lying, unbelieving, accusatory, or adversarial thought that condemns us and looks to kill, steal, and destroy our faith, hope, or love is demonic. This is why we must take every thought captive.

The Lord invites you to submit any intrusive thoughts or words to the Holy Spirit (whether they are your own, from someone else, or from the enemy). When you recognise a negative thought or voice that is affecting you, pray along the following lines: "In the name of Jesus, I take that lie from the enemy captive in Jesus' name. God, what is Your truth for me?" From there, fix your eyes on Jesus and continue to wait on the Lord. He will strengthen and encourage you. As always, Scripture will guide you.

Note: A lie doesn't have power unless we agree with it. The more you hold on to truth, the less room there is for lies to take root. When we submit to God and resist the enemy, he will flee!

I like to keep a journal nearby when I am listening to the Father. In my experience, I find that as I write, the Lord often speaks to me through my thoughts, pictures, or scriptures. If you choose to pray in this manner, I encourage you to write with childlike faith without analysing your words. You can test what you believe you've heard later. Two or three witnesses and scriptural support establish a true word from God.

Remember: God speaks clearly, and He wants you to know His voice!

Invitation to Journey Deeper:

- Spend a moment and ask the Holy Spirit (the Spirit of Truth) to reveal what lies you need to replace with truth. Claim that truth now!
- How does recognising these lies change how you relate to "your" thoughts?

For Further Reading: 2 Corinthians 10:5 and James 4:7

---

1. Mark and Patti Virkler, *4 Keys to Hearing God's Voice* (Shippensburg: Destiny Image Publishers, INC., 2010), 23.

GOD'S VOICE

Now I'll listen carefully for Your voice and wait to hear whatever You say. Let me hear Your promise of peace—the message every one of Your godly lovers longs to hear. Don't let us in our ignorance turn back from following You.

—Psalm 85:8, TPT

There are many ways to hear God's voice. He speaks in stillness, in dreams and visions, through angels, through other people, and through times of worship. He speaks through Scripture, and He speaks through nature. God can speak any way He wants, at any time. If you listen, you will hear Him!

And what does He sound like? Peace, hope, encouragement, and wisdom. His voice fills you with confidence, expectancy, hope, and faith. It convicts and corrects but never condemns. His voice reminds you of who you really are, speaking what we truly need to hear.

Once again, anyone can hear God. Believers and nonbelievers. The same can be said of the enemy; he speaks and anyone can listen. Not all our thoughts are our own. By remaining in the Word of God and knowing how God speaks, we can distinguish between our thoughts, the enemy's voice, and God's voice.

I am constantly shocked that I did not participate in such a wonderful part of the Christian walk for so many years. There are still other times when I am distracted, discouraged, or dissuaded from listening. And even now, I am surprised when I realise I haven't listened and journaled for some time—it brings such life!

There is no better way to start the day than in silence with the Lord, listening for His word and His voice. I cherish this time with the Lord and guard it as a top priority. Sometimes hearing from God is as simple as asking questions and watching for where He moves. Just the other day, God gave me the word "FREEDOM!" for a friend suffering from addiction. When I called to give him the word, he was in total shock and burst into tears. At 6:30 in the morning, he had awakened with me on his mind. The word I gave him was confirmation to take the next step to join an inner-healing ministry. This man is now free from addiction!

God is faithful to answer! His sheep hear His voice! It is God's delight when we listen, and His joy becomes our strength. A small word or encouragement from the Father is all it takes to get us to move from point A to point B. The more time we practice listening, the more in tune we will become throughout each day.

Invitation to Journey Deeper:

- How, where, and when do you hear God's voice most easily? When is it difficult to hear God's voice?
- How has journaling impacted your prayer life?
- Have you ever heard a word from God for someone else? Did you share the word with that person? Why or why not? If you did, how did it go?

For Further Reading: John 14:26-27, Jeremiah 29:11 and Romans 8:1

THE RHEMA WORD OF GOD

In the beginning was the Word, and the Word was with God, and the Word was God.

—John 1:1

The Bible is God's inspired Word. Culture changes, opinions change, but the eternal Word of God never changes. Scripture speaks, instructs, guides, encourages, and matures us through stories, commands, teachings, and the ultimate truth. John 1:1 describes the *logos* Word of God as Jesus Himself.[1]

God also communicates through the *Rhema* Word of God, or when He speaks into our present and very personal circumstances. *Rhema* literally means "an utterance."[2] For instance, the Rhema Word can happen when listening to a sermon or reading a passage of Scripture, and God's Word stands out to you in a new way. God's Word hasn't changed, but He can guide you to apply it to a specific aspect of your life.

When I read the Bible, I try to do so with the awareness that God might intend for a word or story to stand out for my benefit, comfort, or guidance. In these times, it is important to use proper biblical interpretation and not read into the text or make up my own script about what God might be saying. Anyone can pick out a random verse and use it to justify an ungodly position or decision. To confirm what you are hearing truly is from God, it must apply to the same standards of any other prophetic word from God: It must be encouraging, supported by Scripture, confirmed by two or three trusted believers, filled with light, and edifying. God's Word brings life; it can convict but does not condemn. (If you have an orphan lens, His voice may sound condemning. Check yourself often to make sure you are listening through the ears of a son.)

The Holy Spirit has a way of getting our attention through Scripture to guide us in our current circumstances. Along the same lines, God's Rhema Word will come during prayer time as He speaks prophetically through me or others. Rhema Words can be specific and personalized words from God. They can also be scriptures He highlights for us to record, memorize, and regularly meditate on.

God's voice should always move us to act in a way that glorifies His name and continues the process of sanctification. Consider how Jesus was moved to compassion before He released healing on the crowds.

The more time I spend with the Lord, the more Scripture comes alive with meaning and revelation. Really, the more time I spend with the Lord, the more *everything* comes alive. His Word is a lamp for our feet and a light for our path! Now, almost daily, I will hear or read something and it jumps out at me in an entirely new way as I receive new revelation.

Invitation to Journey Deeper:

- Do you believe God speaks into our personal lives and circumstances? Why or why not?
- Have you ever heard the Rhema Word of God? What did He say?
- Before you enter a time of prayer, worship, and study, invite the Holy Spirit to speak to you through His Word. Make a note of anything you hear from the Lord.

For Further Reading: Psalm 119:105 and Matthew 9:36

---

1. *Logos* is a Greek term literally meaning "word" or "speech," and in this case references the Word of God (the Bible).
2. "Logos," *Blue Letter Bible*, accessed February 21, 2022, https://www.blueletter bible.org/lexicon/g4487/niv/mgnt/0-1/.

HEARING GOD

For no matter how many promises God has made, they are "Yes" in Christ. And so through Him the "Amen" is spoken by us to the glory of God.*

—2 Corinthians 1:20

Hearing God's voice takes practice. The more we practice listening, the better listeners we become. In the process, we must risk failure. It's unlikely you'll get it right the first time, and you'll probably miss it countless times after that. But, like any skill worth acquiring, you'll never progress if you don't risk failing.

Risk requires courage, but the reward is great. Practice leads to greater discernment of the still small voice of a very big, gracious God. When we approach God with childlike faith and trust, we become attuned to our Father's voice.

Recently, I was in church when the Lord put a newly married couple on my heart. The Lord's voice and direction were so strong that I had to leave the sanctuary to record what I heard from the Lord and send it to them in bold faith. It was God's grace that I risked sharing what God had put on my heart. The word hit the mark and sent this young couple on a brand new trajectory. Had I not taken the risk, I would not have experienced the blessing of God's word or been able to share it with this couple.

There are also times when I have entirely missed hearing God's voice or mistaken the enemy's voice for His. Satan's voice is deceiving, and even those who have our best interests in mind might not be relying on spiritual guidance or biblical truth. Good intentions don't equal God's will. Our mind, body, or soul can get in the way.

God may not always accomplish His Word the way we think He will, but He will always come through. The more time we spend in His presence, the more we will learn to hear His voice and pray His will. His desires will become our desires. His thoughts will become our thoughts. As we grow to be more like Him, we can trust that His ways are perfect and He is faithful to fulfil His promises.

> *"As the heavens are higher than the earth, so are My ways higher than your ways and My thoughts than your thoughts.*
>
> *—Isaiah 55:9*

A few years ago, I was praying for a baby boy with a severe ongoing and painful bowel disorder. The Lord spoke to my spirit that He would heal the boy. I told the boy's parents, and soon after, the doctors declared the baby was completely healthy. This event greatly encouraged me and filled me with faith. God showed me that I had heard from Him, and He was faithful to do what He said He would do.

Invitation to Journey Deeper:

- How have you seen God answer prayer?
- When has God answered a prayer differently than you expected?
- What bold prayer can you bring to the Lord today?

For Further Reading: Joshua 21:45

DREAMING DREAMS

After this I let my devotion slumber, but my heart for him stayed
awake. I had a dream...

—*Song of Songs* 5:2, TPT

God is sovereign and can speak to us when we are awake *and* asleep.
Our night hours are a special moment of quiet when God can enter our
semi-conscious state and speak to us in unique ways. Sometimes we can
hear things through dreams that we are too distracted to hear when we
are awake. When we sleep, God can speak directly to our hearts in a
unique way since we are less distracted by our own thoughts and other
stimulants (i.e., the noise of daily life).

Dreams can have both literal and metaphorical interpretations. Bibli-
cally speaking, there are examples of both. Scripture records many
instances of God speaking through dreams, including:

- Jacob's dream (Genesis 28:10-22)
- Pharaoh's dream (Genesis 41:1-7)
- The dream Gideon overhears (Judges 7:13-15)
- Daniel's dream (Daniel 4:5)
- The Magi's dream (Matthew 2:12)
- Joseph's dream (Matthew 2:13)

Each of these examples points to a moment in time when God spoke to
an individual through a dream to reveal His plans for the future, give
warning, provide direction or comfort. Some were more veiled and
required interpretation, such as Pharaoh's dream of the fat cattle and
the starving cattle, while others were more direct, such as Joseph's
dream where an angel appeared and told him to take Mary and Jesus to
Egypt.

It is important to note, "Every case of special guidance given to individuals in the Bible has to do with that person's place in the outworking of God's saving purpose."[1] Like the dreamers of the Bible, we must carefully discern and act on our dreams as the Lord instructs. We can also be confident that God does, in fact, speak through our dreams!

Invitation to Journey Deeper:

- Have you ever experienced a dream from the Lord? How did it make you feel?
- When God speaks into your life through dreams, is it easy or difficult for you to act on it?

For Further Reading: Genesis 41:9-13

---

1. Erik Raymond, "What Do We Do with Dreams?" *TGC*, accessed December 30, 2021, https://www.thegospelcoalition.org/blogs/erik-raymond/what-do-we-do-with-dreams/.

INTERPRETING DREAMS PART I

And afterward, I will pour out My Spirit on all people. Your sons and daughters will prophesy, your old men will dream dreams, your young men will see visions.

—Joel 2:28

The interpretation of dreams is both possible and effective. In my own life, God has spoken to me on only a few key occasions through dreams.

Every few months after Abbe died, the Lord gave me a specific dream. In the dream, I would play with Abbe and Bryn when they were quite small (1 and 3, or 2 and 4, respectively). We would wrestle and laugh in the dream, or just enjoy each other's company. Despite their age and the fact that I was asleep, I was fully aware of my current circumstances in life and the loss of Abbe, making our time together that much more special.

In fact, I was completely overwhelmed by the gift of spending time with my daughters. Each time I had this dream, I awoke with tears of joy. God gave me the revelation of the blessing of children through these dreams. As I experienced my children with burning love and deep gratitude, I know I was also experiencing only a small taste of the Father's incredible love for us.

Others have different experiences in their dream lives. I know many prophetic intercessors whom God regularly speaks to through dreams, some even daily. I have a friend who will ask God for wisdom through dreams regarding specific circumstances in his life, and He usually answers! I find it fascinating how God speaks to us all in a unique combination of ways.

Something significant to remember is that, just as in other areas of hearing God's voice, we must use discernment. Dreams are not always from God, as many aspects of our daily lives influence our nighttime hours. Dreams may be your brain processing stress or trauma, or even just mundane day-to-day experiences. Certain medications or foods can also affect dreams. It's even possible that you might have a demonically inspired dream, although this is less common.

Further, the book of Jude teaches about false ministers using God's grace as an excuse for believers to continue sinning. He warns that these men (and subsequently women) will use dreams and visions to deceive God's people and that we should be on guard and prepared to oppose them. What was true then is true today.

Ultimately, the more we focus on Him, the more likely our dreams will be from Him. But just because a dream is "negative" does not mean it is demonic; it could actually still be a message from God. Be careful not to throw these away!

To discern the source of your dream, you must submit *every* dream to God and have a thorough understanding of His Word.

> *Dear friends, do not believe every spirit, but test the spirits to see whether they are from God, because many false prophets have gone out into the world.*
>
> —1 John 4:1

If you happen to have a bad dream that is clearly demonic in nature, seek God's intervention and healing. As you do, be on the lookout for God to move! God promises His beloved sleep in Proverbs 3:24: "When you lie down, you will not be afraid; when you lie down, your sleep will be sweet."

Invitation to Journey Deeper:

- Have you ever had a dream from the Lord? What did He say through it?
- Is there any dream, voice, or word that you need to test against Scripture to ensure it is God-inspired? Take time to study God's Word in light of what you've heard and consider reaching out to a few fellow believers if you need guidance.

For Further Reading: Jude 8 and Deuteronomy 13:1-5

INTERPRETING DREAMS PART II

It is the glory of God to conceal a matter; to search out a matter is the glory of kings.

—Proverbs 25:2

Dream interpretation can be problematic for those not rooted in the Word or connected to the Holy Spirit. If the interpretation is wrong, we can end up making bad decisions or false judgements. In a dream, details are significant and need to be decoded with the help of the Holy Spirit, Scripture, personal experience, and trusted, believing council.[1]

Accurate dream interpretation comes from paying attention to details. There are many believers specifically gifted in this area. It is often helpful to speak through the details of your dream with mature and trusted friends. When you have a notable dream, take a few minutes to write it down. Then, ask yourself questions like:

- What in my life could be influencing this dream?
- Where does this dream take place? How is the setting significant to me?
- What am I feeling in my dream emotionally? What did I feel when I woke up?
- What symbols could God be using in my dream? What do they mean to me?
- What do I think or feel God is saying through my dream? Does this interpretation line up with Scripture?

Now, let's apply these questions to one of the most significant dreams I have had in my life.

In the dream, it was a dark cloudy day, and I was waiting in a long line of homeless men who were hopeless, dirty, dishevelled, and lifeless.

The men entered from outside directly into an individual shower stall. As each man exited the shower, I knelt on the floor, washing their feet. They wore very bright blue suits when they left the room and were clean-cut, confident, and full of life.

- What in my life could be influencing this dream? *I had recently begun serving those suffering from homelessness.*
- Where does this dream take place? How is the setting significant? *The setting was a place where people received cleansing and restoration.*
- What am I feeling in my dream emotionally? What did I feel when I woke up? *I felt hope and life in the dream and woke up filled with compassion.*
- What symbols could God be using in my dream? What do they mean to me? *Footwashing is symbolic of the ministry of Jesus.*
- What do I think or feel God is saying through my dream? Does this interpretation line up with Scripture? *The dream left me in tears and still moves me deeply when I ponder its meaning. I know that it speaks to the formation of Christ within me, and it encouraged me to care for the less fortunate, which had already manifested in many areas of my life. It aligns with John 13:1-17, where Jesus washes the feet of His disciples, setting the ultimate example of humility.*

Dreams are a powerful way for God to connect with our hearts. If you are not a dreamer, I encourage you to ask the Lord to begin speaking to you in the night hours. God wants to speak to you, and the ways in which He can are endless.

Invitation to Journey Deeper:

- Have you ever prayed for God to speak to you through dreams? Ask Him to show you His heart and guide you in your sleep tonight!
- Choose a voice recorder or notepad to keep at your bedside (most phones have options for both); a journal is a great option also. Anytime you have a notable dream, record or jot down the details you remember as soon as you wake up. Then, process through the questions in this section.

For Further Reading: Acts 2:17

---

1. There are many Christian resources on interpreting dreams from God. I personally have gleaned much from Mark Virkler and his daughter Charity's teachings on dreams. I highly recommend reading *Hearing God Through Your Dreams* by Mark Virkler or checking out their videos online.

SPIRITUAL GIFTS

There are different kinds of gifts, but the same Spirit distributes them. There are different kinds of service, but the same Lord. There are different kinds of working, but in all of them and in everyone it is the same God at work.

—1 Corinthians 12:4-6

In 1 Corinthians 12, Paul describes the church as one body with many parts (verse 12). As a body of believers, we are each given specific gifts by the Spirit of God known as *spiritual gifts* intended to edify, encourage, and uphold the body of Christ (verse 7).

To one there is given through the Spirit a message of wisdom, to another a message of knowledge by means of the same Spirit, to another faith by the same Spirit, to another gifts of healing by that one Spirit, to another miraculous powers, to another prophecy, to another distinguishing between spirits, to another speaking in different kinds of tongues, and to still another the interpretation of tongues.

—1 Corinthians 12:8-10

The manifestation of the gifts of the Spirit is to make God known. They serve to equip the saints to edify and unify the church in faith until she comes to a fullness of maturity and harmony of purpose.

It is very rare that people operate in all nine gifts of the Spirit, but it may happen on occasion. Paul encourages us to "... eagerly desire the gifts of the Spirit, especially prophecy," in 1 Corinthians 14:1. But there is something more important than pursuing any gift, and that is the pursuit of love. Without love, and the ability to love others well, we miss the whole point!

If I speak in the tongues of men or of angels, but do not have love, I am only a resounding gong or a clanging cymbal. If I have the gift of prophecy and can fathom all mysteries and all knowledge, and if I have a faith that can move mountains, but do not have love, I am nothing. If I give all I possess to the poor and give over my body to hardship that I may boast, but do not have love, I gain nothing.

—*1 Corinthians 13:1-3*

Understanding the operation, administration, and manifestation of the gifts of the Holy Spirit is a life long journey rooted in love.

1 John 4:16 says, "God is love." We serve a merciful and compassionate God who does all things in love. Since the Father calls us to emulate Him, we must act like Him in love with mercy and grace. When we do, we will see chains broken and lives restored. That is a gift indeed!

Invitation to Journey Deeper:

- What spiritual gifts have you received? Are there any you would like to pray to receive or develop?
- Are you acting in love? What motives spur you on?

For Further Reading: Galatians 5:22-23 and 1 Corinthians 13

LOVE IN ACTION

Love must be sincere. Hate what is evil; cling to what is good. Be devoted to one another in love. Honor one another above yourselves.

—*Romans 12:9-10*

In Luke 10, an expert in the law asks Jesus what he must do to inherit eternal life. Jesus explains that first, he must love the Lord with all his heart, soul, strength, and mind. Second, he must love his neighbour as himself. Jesus goes on to share the parable of the good Samaritan, who cared for a man he found beaten on the side of the road when no one else would.

> *"Which of these three do you think was a neighbor to the man who fell into the hands of robbers?" The expert in the law replied, "The one who had mercy on him." Jesus told him, "Go and do likewise."*

—*Luke 10:36-37*

Just as God is not passive, standing removed from our lives, neither is His love. Romans 12:9-10 serves as a reminder not just to use the spiritual gifts God has given us, but of what it looks like to use them *in love*.

Love according to worldly standards is a feeling. It tells us only those who earn love get love, and therefore we should be selective about who receives it. That usually equals loving only when it's easy or feels good, or "falling out of love" during difficult times or after a betrayal. Love is a choice, not always a feeling.

There have been many times when acting in love was not what I wanted to do. It would have been much easier to just move on or pray for the person in front of me who, to the world's standards, was unlovable. One time, in particular, the Lord provoked me to move, not based on how I felt (I had a terrible attitude), but based on what He wanted.

As I moved in obedience, He increased my compassion, and I connected with the person relationally in love to serve and encourage. It was God's love moving through me, not my love based on feelings.

Scripture teaches us about true love. It is not always easy and often pushes us out of our comfort zones. Love takes hold of our pride and points us and others back to Jesus. It causes us to rely on His strength instead of our own. The kind of love God calls us to, His love, is only possible when we rely on the One who *is* love.

Invitation to Journey Deeper:

- Is it easy or hard for you to love others? How can you love your enemies?
- What does love in action look like in your life? How is God calling you to grow in this area?

For Further Reading: Luke 6:32

Part Three

Abiding in Christ

God designed us with purpose. First, to love God. Second, to love others as ourselves. The Father calls us to "abide" or to be in relationship with Him. From that intimate connection, He will transform us in a way that brings heaven to earth, loving in a way that points others back to Him.

Abiding moves us past knowing *about* Him and helps us become *like* Him through relationship *with* Him. As we abide in Him, we will bear much fruit. Apart from the vine (Jesus), the branches (you and me) can do nothing. What can a branch do when cut off from a vine? Nothing! We must be connected to the source of life to bear fruit.[1]

The more we let go, the more we trust God and spend time in His presence, the more He transforms our body, soul, and spirit. The finished work of the cross and our completeness in Him is our reality.

As we awaken to who we are in Christ through the renewing of our minds, we discover our new creation life! With Him, fields once barren and fruitless will begin to bear much spiritual fruit reflecting His nature and work in us. John 15:8 says that "This is to My Father's glory, that you bear much fruit, showing yourselves to be My disciples."

Fruit from abiding looks like producing other disciples, transformed lives, and the fruit of the spirit: love, joy, peace, patience, kindness, goodness, gentleness, and self-control.[2]

This section invites you from a place of knowing God into a place of abiding in Him to bear fruit. It outlines the sanctification process, a process of maturing that begins with surrendering our old selves that lived according to the ways of the world, choosing instead to trust our Father whose ways are higher than our ways. It encourages you to pursue the deeper things of God that result in bearing good fruit. God bless you on the journey!

----

1. John 15:1-8
2. Galatians 5:22-23

IT'S ALL A GIFT

So if the Son sets you free from sin, then become a true son and be unquestionably free!

—John 8:36, TPT

Many of us in the West have everything we need to survive comfortably. We rely on a façade of success as our source of security and to bolster our egos instead of seeking after God to meet our deeper needs. It is easy to think that we earned or deserve what we have and forget that everything is a gift.

The air we breathe, the food we eat, the beauty of nature, the sunshine, our health, our work, our time on this earth, this day, all the way to our eternal salvation… these are all gifts from God, and our response should be continual thanksgiving. Knowing this gives a whole new perspective to John 15:5, which ends, "apart from Me you can do nothing." *We only have what He gives.* All blessings are from Him, the Father of lights. EVERYTHING we have that is good is from God; He is the source of all provision.

Every living creature is alive only because of the *ruach* or "breath of God".[1] In Him, we live, we move and have our being. In the second chapter of Genesis, God blew life into Adam's nostrils, giving him breath. We breathe because God breathed life into us. When we breathe, we are breathing in the Spirit of God. Every breath is a gift from God. (This reality explains why many in the New Age focus on their breath. Even *they* recognise the importance of it! And so should we!)

In the natural realm, we need to eat and drink. In the spirit realm, Jesus is the bread and the blood. Our spirit feeds on Him. Jesus' words are spirit and life. "Just as the living Father sent me and I live because of the Father, so the one who feeds on me will live because of me," John

6:57. Feast on the thoughts of Christ and maintain Christ consciousness.

God delights in showing mercy. Righteousness comes *only* because of our belief in Jesus and our submission to Him. The greater the sin, the greater His grace. Compared to our Holy God, the forgiveness we receive is incomprehensible! He who is forgiven much loves much. We were once sinners. Now, we are saved by grace and are saints, born again and one with God. His righteousness is now ours as we are in Christ! Of course, we are all works in progress, becoming more like Him as we pursue Him each day. Grace is not a license to sin but the empowerment to overcome sin!

Dean Briggs, an intercessory missionary, preacher, and author, lays out five tips on aligning our lives with God and living in the fullness of His grace:

1. THANK GOD for the price He paid for you. God declares over you what He declares over Jesus in Matthew 3:17 "...This is My Son, whom I love; with Him I am well pleased."
2. DELIGHT IN GOD and get personal. Talk to Him. Spend time with Him. When you wake up, say, "Good morning, Holy Spirit, Jesus, and Father!"
3. ABIDE IN JESUS and stay connected throughout your day. As you walk with Him, you become more like Him. Rest in His presence.
4. OBEY THE HOLY SPIRIT and learn to hear His still small voice.
5. KNOW THE WORD OF GOD and let the truth cut through lies and renew your mind.

God's grace has nothing to do with what we have done and everything to do with what He has already done for us. Because of Jesus' finished work on the cross as the ultimate and final sacrifice, we are totally free! We simply receive all Jesus has done for us through faith.

We can truly love God and others from the source of His perfect love! As we pursue Him, we experience the fullness of a God who loves His children unconditionally, offering peace now and for all eternity. Grace encourages, corrects, comforts, strengthens, and empowers us to become more like Jesus. Our only job is to believe and receive, remembering that everything truly is a gift.

Invitation to Journey Deeper:

- What areas of your life have you forgotten to thank God for?
- When you thank Him, how does this change your perspective on God's grace?
- Do you walk in the Lord's mercy and grace, or are you carrying the weight of your sin?
- You were created for love. Pause and ponder this incredible truth, and simply receive His love.

For Further Reading: Acts 17:28, Genesis 2:7, Luke 7:47 and John 15

---

1. "Ruach," *Blue Letter Bible*, accessed February 21, 2022, https://www.blueletter bible.org/lexicon/h7307/kjv/wlc/o-1/.

LETTING GO, LETTING GOD

Laying your life down in tender surrender before the Lord will bring life, prosperity, and honor as your reward.

—Proverbs 22:4, TPT

If sin separates us from God, then repentance and surrender bring us back to the truth of our union with Him. By acknowledging and admitting our failings, where we have *missed the mark*, we put God back in His rightful place as Lord and King of our lives. It is there that we find true refreshment, joy, and rest. Jesus tells us in Scripture:

> *"As the Father has loved Me, so have I loved you. Now remain in My love. If you keep My commands, you will remain in My love, just as I have kept My Father's commands and remain in His love. I have told you this so that My joy may be in you and that your joy may be complete."*
>
> —John 15:9-11

Humbling ourselves by first repenting of sin and then surrendering everything to God allows us to experience the glorious freedom He offers.

When we surrender our lives to Jesus, we turn our will and ourselves over to the care of our loving heavenly Father. By doing so, we leave behind the cares of the world: fear, worry, anxiety, control, addictions, stress, negativity, sin, doubts, and our past. While the word "surrender" can have a negative connotation akin to "giving up" or failing, the biblical model of surrender is not about losing. It's about *winning*. In fact, Jesus reveals His glory through our surrendered lives.

Take My yoke upon you and learn from Me, for I am gentle and humble in heart, and you will find rest for your souls.

—Matthew 11:29

Surrender is an ongoing process of going deeper and growing in faith, trust, and maturity (love is the ultimate mark of maturity!). Like Jesus in Luke 22:42, surrender says, "not My will, but Yours be done." It replaces our worries and fears with peace and joy. I can't count the number of times I have cast my cares, anxieties, and failures on the Lord and received His peace, comfort, and reassurance in return. A posture of letting go releases us from the sin and fear that binds us, ultimately uniting us with God.

Beloved friends, what should be our proper response to God's marvelous mercies? To surrender yourselves to God to be His sacred, living sacrifices. And live in holiness, experiencing all that delights His heart. For this becomes your genuine expression of worship.

—Romans 12:1, TPT

To surrender is to coin the common yet powerful phrase, "let go and let God." Over time, as I have let go, my desires have aligned with His desires. Many things that used to matter and seem so important no longer have any pull on or power over me. As a living sacrifice, my life is His, and I live and die *for Him.* I am not my own. It is no longer I who lives, but Christ in me; fear has lost its hold as I am God's, and His perfect love casts out all fear. I have found rest for my soul. I have found Jesus. When I feel the cares of this world beginning to mount, I know it is time to release them back to God and abide.

We all have areas that require "letting go" in order to receive greater freedom. Let go of everything, including what you consider good. This positions us to be in a place of obedience and expectation, where God carries the weight instead of us! When you give God what you are holding onto, you will receive all He has for you. Open your hands in surrender to the Father. Feel the freedom of His Spirit taking your burdens. Repent when needed, surrender all, and receive the gift of His gentle and easy yoke.

Invitation to Journey Deeper:

- What sin do you need to repent of in order to surrender your life more fully to God?
- Is there something *good* in your life that is actually impeding your relationship with the Lord? Look at your life. What are you holding onto (good or bad) that the Lord is asking you to let go of? (i.e., work, a leadership role outside of your family, the past, volunteering, money, etc.)
- Is there an area of your life you have a difficult time surrendering to the Lord? Why is it challenging for you?

For Further Reading: Matthew 11:30

ALL THINGS FOR GOOD

And we know that in all things God works for the good of those who love Him, who have been called according to His purpose.

—Romans 8:28

Despite the hurts and traumas we have all faced, Scripture is clear that God works all things together for good. We cannot love our enemies by our own will—it takes the love of God. Only when Jesus truly becomes the King of our hearts can we love all people. Nothing can stop His plans and purposes for our lives if we choose to trust Him. This is wonderful as those who are forgiven much, love much!

We must have mercy on others as God has mercy on us.

One afternoon in 2017, I was at my office when I received a call from my daughter, Bryn, and her therapist from the addiction centre. She had a breakthrough in therapy and was ready to share a very dark secret. Bryn told me that someone I was very close with had seriously abused her *for years*. My world came to a complete stop.

When we got off the phone, I sat at my desk and cried throughout the afternoon and into the night. Thankfully, this person had been out of our lives for a long time, but the damage they left was still very present and ongoing. I felt a deep sense of pain and regret. How could I have missed what was going on? How was I so distracted? I got down on my knees, crying out in shame and repentance.

As I processed everything that I had just learnt, I was horrified. I felt something close to hatred attempt to enter my heart. Immediately, I voiced my forgiveness and released this person through tears and anger, even though I didn't want to. I certainly didn't feel like forgiving this person, but I would not give the enemy any more room to wreak havoc in my life.

This specific process of forgiveness began with my will and eventually moved into my heart. This person abused both my daughters, forming a primary root of trauma that led to addiction and many destructive behaviours in their lives. I had to forgive over and over as the damage from one person manifested repeatedly in my daughters' lives.

Whenever I feel my heart harden or resentment or anger begins to rise, I engage in forgiveness towards others and towards myself in order to enjoy great freedom.

> "To be a Christian means to forgive the inexcusable because God has forgiven the inexcusable in you."
>
> —C.S.Lewis[1]

Invitation to Journey Deeper:

- When was the last time someone forgave you for a wrong you committed against them? How did that make you feel?
- Which aspect of forgiveness do you struggle with most? Why?
- How does the act of forgiveness impact you? How does it set you free?

For Further Reading: Jeremiah 29:11

---

1. "Forgiving the Inexcusable," Right from the heart.org, accessed March 18, 2022, https://rightfromtheheart.org/devotions/forgiving-the-inexcusable/.

FORGIVENESS

For if you forgive other people when they sin against you, your heavenly Father will also forgive you.

—Matthew 6:14

To repent and ask God for forgiveness requires the heart position of submission and humility. When we ask for forgiveness, God grants our requests. He asks us to do the same for others.

By forgiving, we have the privilege of living in God's grace and the freedom it brings. Forgiveness is our charge and responsibility as believers. It won't always be easy, especially at first, or if you've been harbouring resentment or bitterness towards someone for a long time. Forgiveness is a choice that leads to peace, health, and freedom. To forgive often requires daily action, sometimes moment-by-moment surrender. In time, this posture softens our hearts towards others and becomes easier.

Whenever I feel judgement, resentment, or anger well up against a person, I must choose to move into forgiveness. To do so, I position myself to forgive them for what they did, the impact their actions had on me and/or my family, and how their actions made me feel. Then I declare a blessing over the person. Eventually, my heart softens, and I maintain a position of freedom in Christ.

Scripture is even so specific as to remind us how *often* we should forgive. In Matthew 18, Peter asks Jesus how many times he should forgive his brother who sins against him, suggesting up to seven times. However, in verse 22, "Jesus answered, 'I tell you, not seven times, but seventy-seven times.'" Some translations suggest He actually said seventy *times* seven. That's 490 times! Jesus wasn't being literal here but was pointing to forgiveness with no limits.

When you forgive, invite Jesus into the process and declare it with your mouth. Forgive the person for what they did and then for how it affected you and made you feel. Release them from all judgement, and then bless them! Continue to pray for that person as the Lord leads. Jesus commands in Luke 6:28 to "bless those who curse you, pray for those who mistreat you." The Holy Spirit may also ask you to bless the person with no expectations regarding their response or reaction to your goodwill. This is how we plant Kingdom seeds. This is freedom!

After Jesus told Peter how to forgive, He told him the parable of the unmerciful servant. In the story, a servant could not repay his debts to the king, so he begged for mercy, which he received. The king mercifully cancelled his debt and sent the man home. However, upon his release, the servant found one of his fellow servants who owed *him* money. When the fellow servant could not pay the debt, the king's servant had him sent to jail. When the king found what had gone down, he was furious and sent the unmerciful servant to jail to be tortured until he paid off his debt.

Just like the king in the parable, our king, the King of kings, forgave us *much*. God asks us to forgive those who owe us in the same way. May we share the forgiveness we have received with those who have sinned against us as the Father forgave us.

Invitation to Journey Deeper:

- Is it easy or hard for you to forgive others? Why?
- What does it look like to forgive with no limits? What changes when you invite Jesus into the process of forgiveness?
- Ask the Holy Spirit to reveal how much you have been forgiven. How does this change your thinking about freely forgiving others?

For Further Reading: Matthew 6:12 and Romans 10:17

A BIBLICAL APPROACH TO
FORGIVENESS

We all have people to forgive. Family, friends, and strangers can hurt us intentionally or unintentionally. Sometimes we need to practice receiving forgiveness from God for the sins we have committed. Either way, the process of forgiveness is one we should be familiar with and practice regularly.

Hebrews 12:15 instructs: "See to it that no one falls short of the grace of God and that no bitter root grows up to cause trouble and defile many." The more we forgive (and let go of the resentment, anger, and bitterness that accompanies unforgiveness), the more we will grow spiritually and receive God's promise of peace and joy.

Often, people are reluctant to forgive because they have confused forgiveness with trust. You can forgive someone who hurt you without trusting them again. Forgiveness is a gift. Trust is earned. If someone has broken trust, it may take years for them to earn it back. In fact, they may never earn it back! But that does not mean we should not forgive them. Paul commands us to forgive in Colossians 3:13, "Bear with each other and forgive one another if any of you has a grievance against someone. Forgive as the Lord forgave you."

Consider the steps on the following pages to guide you through the forgiveness process. Lean on God and His Word to lead you and give you strength each step of the way.

STEPS TO FORGIVENESS

1. Acknowledge your pain. If you need to, write down what happened and be honest about your emotions.

2. Imagine being in the shoes of the person who hurt you. Remember how God forgave you and commands you to forgive others.

3. Forgive the person who hurt you.

4. Let go of your pain and determine to move forward in your thoughts and life.

5. Pray for the person who hurt you, as Jesus commands us to in Matthew 5:44.

6. Forgiveness can be a process. Continue to forgive as emotions or thoughts come up.

Forgiveness is a choice, not a feeling. However, feelings can be an indicator of your level of forgiveness. Ultimately, the choice to forgive is not about whether the person deserves it or even if the other person will participate in the exchange (sometimes it's better and safer if they don't!). God requires us to forgive.

Forgiveness brings healing and freedom. The Bible tells us our war is not against flesh and blood but against powers and principalities. It doesn't mean the person is not responsible or accountable for their choices, but we must know who the real enemy is. God is the ultimate judge; we are not. Our choice to forgive reflects our deeper choice to align with the kingdom of heaven.

Forgiveness must be specific. Forgiveness should include specifics on what your offenders have done and how they made you feel. Choose to forgive your offenders in specific areas and then speak peace and blessing over them, declaring your freedom from bondage and bitterness in Jesus' name.

Forgive from your heart. True forgiveness puts God in His rightful place as the King of our hearts and lives. By choosing not to forgive, we give the person we hold bitterness toward control over our emotions and thoughts. If you are struggling to forgive, ask the Holy Spirit to remove any unrighteous anger, resentment, bitterness, and judgement from your heart and replace it with compassion.

Forgiveness ends in blessing. Remember to bless whoever hurt you. Blessing softens our hearts and brings healing to them and to us, opening the door for God to move. Jesus said to bless those who curse you!

RECIEVING FORGIVENESS

In Him we have redemption through His blood, the forgiveness of sins, in accordance with the riches of God's grace that He lavished on us. With all wisdom and understanding, He made known to us the mystery of His will according to His good pleasure, which He purposed in Christ.

—Ephesians 1:7-9

Forgiveness releases us from guilt and shame. I carried regret and shame for the abortion my girlfriend had while at university (she later became the mother of my two daughters). Later in life, I unknowingly exposed my daughters to a child abuser. I have made poor decisions as a friend, parent, and businessman. The list is endless.

Forgiving others who sin against me has always been easier than receiving God's forgiveness for my own sin. It wasn't until 2016 that I started to understand how ungodly beliefs around not being enough provided the foundation for my inability to receive God's forgiveness through His grace. I used to think freedom came by forgiving myself but we cannot forgive our own sin. *Only Jesus can forgive sin.* Only God's forgiveness heals and frees us! Even if we have to deal with the natural consequences of sin, His grace enables us to do so well.

Continuing to hold on to my past mistakes and missteps would have kept me from living in the full freedom God offers through forgiveness. I would have missed the point of the cross.

When Jesus was crucified on the cross and rose from the dead three days later, He became the ultimate sacrifice for our sin. We no longer have to carry the weight of our past because it died with Him that day. Instead, we are free to live in the glory of our Redeemer who lives!

The more I exercise this muscle of receiving God's forgiveness and forgiving others, the stronger it gets. Not only that, but it serves as a reminder of the work Jesus did on the cross for me and my brothers and sisters in Christ. I am free because He loves us so much.

Every good and perfect gift is from above, coming down from the Father of the heavenly lights, who does not change like shifting shadows.

—James 1:17

How fair would it be for me to deny or return a gift from my Father in heaven? So it is with the gift of forgiveness. Let's receive this precious gift today and every day.

Invitation to Journey Deeper:

- Is it easy or difficult for you to receive forgiveness? Why?
- How would your life be different if you received God's forgiveness more easily?
- How would your life be different if you could forgive others more easily?

For Further Reading: Ephesians 2:13 and Matthew 9:4-8

THE GIFT OF FAITH

Now to each one the manifestation of the Spirit is given for the common good. To one there is given through the Spirit a message of wisdom, to another a message of knowledge by means of the same Spirit, to another faith by the same Spirit, to another gifts of healing by that one Spirit, to another miraculous powers, to another prophecy, to another distinguishing between spirits, to another speaking in different kinds of tongues, and to still another the interpretation of tongues. All these are the work of one and the same Spirit, and He distributes them to each one, just as He determines.

—*1 Corinthians 12:7-11*

Faith comes from hearing the Word of God. As we continually hear the Word, faith grows. A measure of faith is given to every person. This enables them to respond to God and receive salvation. This is "saving faith" and is accessed through grace.

As an engineer, I defaulted to reason and human understanding before I knew God. I spent a lot of energy trying to bring God down to my level. This was an attempt to make God my equal. I was drowning in a sea of pride and needed someone to rescue me.

Thank God for His relentless pursuit of me! God rescued me from my sin and brokenness, and the more time I spent with Him and in His Word, the more He filled me with faith. Disciplining myself to lean not on my understanding does not come naturally to me, but with my eyes fixed on Jesus, I am growing! Instead of floundering in the wake of life, I now have an anchor to hold on to.

> "Faith is the most powerful of all forces operating in humanity and when you have it in depth nothing can get you down."
>
> —Norman Vincent Peale[1]

Through abiding, I now understand that God is incomprehensible to the human mind. The more I know Him, the more I realise how much more there is to know! I will never fully comprehend all of His ways. However, I can trust Him, despite not understanding how He is working. With each step of faith, God has shown up and reminded me He is, in fact, very alive and very good. I regularly ask God to continue to grow my faith and to deliver me from unbelief, and I encourage you to do the same. Praise God for the gift of faith! With faith, everything changes! Faith is the currency of heaven!

Invitation to Journey Deeper:

- What is one step of faith you have taken where you then saw God show up?
- Does faith or reason come more naturally to you? What are the positives and negatives of both?
- Why has God given us both the ability to reason and have faith?

For Further Reading: James 2:18, Hebrews 11:32-33 and Romans 12:3

---

1. "Norman Vincent Peale Quotes," *Self Help Daily*, accessed January 7, 2022, https://www.selfhelpdaily.com/motivational-quotes/norman-vincent-peale-quotes/.

A POSTURE OF SURRENDER

Repent, then, and turn to God, so that your sins may be wiped out, that times of refreshing may come from the Lord.

—Acts 3:19

Repentance, if you remember, is translated from the Greek word *metanoia* in the New Testament. It means "to change the mind... It has to do with the way you think about something. You've been thinking one way, but now you think the opposite way."[1] But to repent goes beyond thinking. True repentance results in changed behaviours. As we align our thinking with God, our behaviours naturally follow.

Acts 3:19 essentially says: *change your mind, and then turn to God.* Repentance changes how we think, act, feel, perceive, and function. If our realisation of what is right and true does not result in actual life change, then what good is it? Real repentance:

...transforms the heart
...aligns us with God
...is an act of obedience
...sanctifies us
...produces humility
...obliterates shame and guilt
...enables us to live in God's grace
...changes our thinking and behaviours

None of these characteristics are passive. This is because repentance invites us into a lifestyle of surrender and obedience, which creates a hunger for the truth that requires action. We receive righteousness and salvation through our one-time confession of faith in Jesus. Salvation is ours if we choose to accept it. Repentance, however, is a part of the ongoing process of sanctification. Doing so moulds us into the image of Jesus as we work out our salvation with fear and trembling.

Receiving God's gift of salvation begins with acknowledging our sin and our need for a saviour. The result of giving our lives to Jesus, repenting, and living lives of faith enables God's grace to continuously transform us into the likeness of Christ.

The Holy Spirit convicts, leading to godly sorrow, resulting in repentance which establishes our victory. God sees us through the finished work of the cross. His Word confirms our identity and how He sees us (read *Song of Songs*, an incredible book that describes God's love in poetic form). In any area of our lives where we do not have the mind of Christ, we must repent and realign by His grace.

Invitation to Journey Deeper:

- Are you living a lifestyle of repentance? How does this play out in your daily life?
- What might God be asking you to turn away from?
- Are you connected to other believers who encourage you, strengthen you, hold you accountable, and agree with the truth of the Word of God? How can you further invest in the body of Christ?

For Further Reading: Philemon 2:21 and Philippians 2:12

---

1. "What Is Repentance? How Do We Repent and Become Saved?" *Christianity*, accessed January 7, 2022, https://www.christianity.com/jesus/following-jesus/repentance-faith-and-salvation/what-does-it-mean-to-repent.html.

SANCTIFICATION

Consecrate yourselves and be holy, because I am the Lord your God. Keep My decrees and follow them. I am the Lord, who makes you holy.

—*Leviticus* 20:7-8

To be sanctified is to be set apart and used for the Lord's purposes. Set apart from the world, and set apart for the Kingdom. Sanctification is the continual process of becoming more like Christ (growing in spiritual maturity and being filled with Him) as we submit our lives to Him daily. This is how we work out our salvation with fear and trembling. Our spirit is perfected but our soul needs to be brought into divine alignment. Again, love is the ultimate purpose and indicator of maturity. The shed blood of Jesus makes us holy the moment we declare His name and make Him Lord and Saviour of our lives. We become more like Jesus with each opportunity we take to set ourselves aside and choose His ways over our own.

"Sanctification is possessing the mind of Christ."

—John G. Lake[1]

To live in a state of grace comes from living in a state of repentance. A repentant heart feels sorrow for the sins we commit, which leads us back to God. Jesus defeated sin and paid our debt in full on the cross! When we submit to Him, it puts us on the highway of holiness. The more we become like Him, the more we understand His ways, experience His peace, wisdom, and glorious freedom that comes from surrendering our lives to the One who reigns over the heavens and the earth. His ways are higher than our ways.

Jesus showed the ultimate act of surrender on the cross. Surrender is giving ourselves over to God. It's the part where we turn to Him with open hands, saying less of me, more of You. It invites us into the transformation process that allows God to work in and through us. In surrender, we acknowledge our dependence on God, letting go of a life centred on the self, and in its place, we discover *abundant life.*

Through the sanctification process, you will notice that there will be selflessness where there once was selfishness. Where there once was judgement, there will be grace and mercy. Love will replace hate, and truth will replace lies. We will no longer see things through a worldly lens. We will see things (and people) through the eyes of Jesus. The more we surrender to the sanctification process, the more our outer lives will reflect the inner transformation of being made in Christ's image and being used for His glory.

Invitation to Journey Deeper:

- How has God transformed you to become more like Him?
- Who do you know that has experienced a dramatic life transformation because of his/her willingness to pursue God and submit to Him?

For Further Reading: John 3:30, Proverbs 16:17, Philippians 2:12 and 1 Thessalonians 5:23

---

1. John G. Lake, "Sanctification of Spirit, Soul and Body," *Healing Room Ministries,* accessed January 7, 2021, https://healingrooms.com/about/johnGLake/?document=114.

RESTING IN HIM

The Lord will fight for you; you need only to be still.

—Exodus 14:14

Do you live in a state of surrender or striving? Surrender results in rest. From rest, we can do whatever God asks of us with peace and joy. Working from our own strength and strife results in burnout.

Avoiding rest is often a way to avoid facing our faults and things that need to be dealt with in our own lives. The flesh always wants to perform, but the spirit simply "is." Rest is of the Spirit. By staying busy, we stay distracted, living in a state of ignorance, numbing, or disbelief. Slowing down often results in letting our flaws rise to the surface (sins, hurts, unforgiveness, traumas, poor boundaries, people-pleasing, etc.). Silence and rest can leave us feeling vulnerable and raw.

When we finally pause long enough to let our minds, bodies, and souls rest in the still and quiet of God's presence, we hear His voice. That's where He calls us to become more like Him. But Satan wants to keep us busy. Distraction stunts our growth and encourages a lifestyle of independence from God. Rest breathes life into our tired bodies, reminding us that our strength comes from the Lord.

Rest does not equal laziness. It also goes far beyond not working or working. As believers, we are called to work out of a place of rest. That means we work appropriately within healthy boundaries, honouring God's command to take a day off (to take a sabbath). It means that we do our daily tasks without accepting anxiety or strife. Our source of strength and success comes from abiding in His presence, the ultimate form of rest.

Rest expresses our faith and trust in God. One expression of death to self is stillness and silence, giving our time and attention to God, resting in Him. Anything done in the flesh, even if it appears good, will not result in Kingdom fruit. The amount of activities or busyness you engage in does not mean you are accomplishing anything. True accomplishment comes from focusing on His priorities.

Making God our ultimate priority will always result in fruitful accomplishments without striving. As Hebrews 4:10 says in *The Passion Translation*, "As we enter into God's faith-rest life we cease from our own works, just as God celebrates His finished works and rests in them."

In surrender, God promises rest. The more we surrender to Him and let go of our attempts to control our lives and the lives of others, the more joy and freedom we find. The joy of the Lord is our strength. It delivers a crippling blow to the attempts of the enemy to dissuade us from our calling by keeping us focused on what God is doing.

> "Rest is a weapon against the enemy. He cannot penetrate your peace."
>
> —Graham Cooke[1]

Surrender is only possible if we are "dead to self" because our flesh rebels against God. Opening the door to His Spirit, closes the door to our flesh.

I find that, just like with repentance, surrender is an ongoing process. Depending on the day, it may be something big or small. Whenever anything becomes a burden, or you lose your peace, those are indicators to give whatever "it" is over to the Lord. There is always a release in surrender, which yields greater trust and peace as we stop striving and enter His presence.

Invitation to Journey Deeper:

- How do you typically view rest? What place does it hold in your life?
- Do you feel rested? What burden does God want to carry for you?
- If you are a believer and are tired, burdened, or exhausted, refer back to the section in Part 1 (pages 82-95) on the religious spirit as a refresher on how to receive God's grace and freedom.

For Further Reading: Exodus 20:8, Matthew 11:29 and Nehemiah 8:10

---

1. Graham Cooke, "Rest is a Weapon," *Brilliant Perspectives*, accessed January 7, 2021, https://brilliantperspectives.com/rest-is-a-weapon/.

REST AS WORSHIP

"I am the Lord, the God of all mankind. Is anything too hard for Me?"

—Jeremiah 32:27

Leaning into God's rest is an act of worship. It moves us from "doing" to "being," from depending on our own strength to depending on God's. "Being" makes it about *Him* and not about us. As an entrepreneur, learning how to rest has been challenging. Thankfully, it's a battle God is winning, and I am learning how to trust and surrender in deeper ways than I knew was possible. By His grace, I am learning how to "be" and not just "do." I am learning how to worship through rest.

Rest destroys any impulse to take the glory for what God has done. All urgency, rush, stress, and panic come from human striving. God is never in a rush or in a panic. Rest is a gift but is also a discipline. The more uncomfortable we are in this space, the more we need it. In rest, we affirm our trust in Him and His abilities, not our own. As we focus on Him, this act of obedience and reverence builds intimacy and transforms us from the inside out. Rest does not mean we do nothing (although ceasing all activity is also important sometimes), but that we operate in *shalom*. Shalom is peace AND harmony AND wholeness AND completeness AND security. *Shalom* is the fruit of abiding in His presence.

Rest is so important that God made it a commandment. On the seventh day of creation, God rested from all the work He had done the previous six days. God then tells the Israelites in Exodus 20:8-10, "Remember the Sabbath day by keeping it holy. Six days you shall labor and do all your work, but the seventh day is a sabbath to the Lord your God. On it you shall not do any work, neither you, nor your son or daughter, nor your male or female servant, nor your animals, nor any foreigner residing in your towns." Then He blessed the sabbath, making it a holy day. From Friday sundown to Saturday sundown, He commands us to follow His example and rest from our labours.

Jesus encourages us to take the concept of rest into our labours. We are to "work out of rest." I love sabbath! I realise God can do more in my rest as I honour Him than I could ever do in my most productive moments. Jesus redeemed and removed the toil and the sweat of *our* brows when His brow was pierced. Yes, God is that good. Jesus redeemed everything, including our pain.

Rest honours God and is an opportunity to focus on God and family. Jesus rested. Therefore, we should make every effort to follow His lead as an act of obedience. Consider the ways Jesus rested: Jesus slept in the middle of a storm; Jesus rested after performing miracles; Jesus spent time in solitude with God before choosing the disciples; Jesus encouraged the disciples to rest with Him; and Jesus withdrew to pray before His arrest.

The good news is that this discipline not only glorifies God but also brings refreshment to our souls. God takes our anxieties, fears, and troubles and grants us peace and joy. Humility and rest go hand in hand. Humility comes from a heart of complete surrender and dependence on God. In our weakness, His strength is perfected. No longer do we have to bear our own burdens. We can find rest in Him.

Invitation to Journey Deeper:

- Is rest easy or difficult for you? Why?
- When you rest, is it a rest that honours God or are you keeping yourself distracted from hearing His voice?
- How can you practice a posture of rest while at work?

For Further Reading: Genesis 2:2; 2:3, Hebrews 4:10-11, Matthew 8:24; 14:22-23, Luke 6:12-13; 22:44. Mark 6:30-32 and 1 Corinthians 12:9

JOURNEY TO REST

Give God the right to direct your life, and as you trust Him along the way, you'll find He pulled it off perfectly!

—*Psalms 37:5, TPT*

True rest is impossible for Christians living under an orphan spirit or a spirit of religion. Rest is natural for sons and daughters. For some, rest might feel intimidating. For others, it may feel impossible. Regardless, *God will always meet you there.* And like most things, the more you do it, the easier it will become.

The good news is that Scripture tells us the key to finding rest clearly in Matthew 11:28-30, when Jesus says, "Come to Me, all you who are weary and burdened, and I will give you rest. Take My yoke upon you and learn from Me, for I am gentle and humble in heart, and you will find rest for your souls. For My yoke is easy and My burden is light." And in Hebrews 4:11, which states, "Let us, therefore, make every effort to enter that rest, so that no one will perish by following their example of disobedience."

The ultimate destination of resting in God's love is the ability to love others. From rest, we can love and bless others as they experience Jesus in us. The more we rest in His love, the more we can love others without strife or fear. Love is the overflow, not the reaction. The enemy loves to keep us busy and distracted. He knows that when we spend time in rest, then we've given God control of our lives—the opposite of what he wants. Satan doesn't want us to love others or experience God's love for us! This shows how important it is to slow down and let God do what He does best!

As you begin your journey of learning to rest, it might be helpful to process through some of the unique challenges that prevent you from experiencing true rest. Understanding your struggles and submitting them to the Lord will help you keep your guard up when Satan tries to tempt you. Even Jesus rested, and so should we.

Invitation to Journey Deeper:

Set aside some time to read and think through the questions below. Write your answers in a journal, a note on your phone, or another safe place as you reflect on what it looks like to practice a lifestyle of repentance, surrender, and rest.

- When was the last time you truly rested?
- How can you incorporate a rhythm of rest into your life?
- What burden have you been holding onto that you need to surrender to God?
- Where do you need to let go of control and let God take the lead?

For Further Reading: Psalm 62:1 and 2 Samuel 7:11

FILLED WITH GRACE

Do not take revenge, my dear friends, but leave room for God's wrath, for it is written: "It is Mine to avenge; I will repay," says the Lord.

—Romans 12:19

Bryn bravely walked in forgiveness towards those who hurt her, including me, and I am truly grateful for that. If she had chosen not to forgive, her heart would have remained closed to God. She would not have received healing on such a deep level. And she might very well still be in a place of sadness and deep pain. However, because she has chosen to walk in forgiveness, she is also walking in joy, freedom, and hope. She is close to God, and because of that, she and I are closer than ever. Beauty, sweetness, and grace fill her life.

Bryn went from a totally self-focused young woman to a mature adult, living far away from home doing the Lord's work. She spends her time learning the Bible and ministering to orphans and families. All of this is happening because of the radical life change that came from her seeking God. *That* is the power of forgiveness. It opens the door to true life transformation on a level like no other.

Harbouring unforgiveness is like ingesting poison, all the while hoping the person who hurt you dies. We can choose not to forgive, but we will wind up doing ourselves more damage than good in the end. Unforgiveness binds us through an ungodly soul-tie or an unhealthy connection to someone else. Unforgiveness tethers us to judgement, a role reserved only for God.

God's judgement, contrary to man's judgement, is perfectly just. His ways are higher than ours as He sees the desires of the heart and depth of human struggle from an eternal perspective. Our view is one-dimensional and often self-serving. As people disappoint, we must look beyond the person to remember the work of Jesus on the cross.

All of us also lived among them at one time, gratifying the cravings of our flesh and following its desires and thoughts. Like the rest, we were by nature deserving of wrath. But because of His great love for us, God, who is rich in mercy, made us alive with Christ even when we were dead in transgressions—it is by grace you have been saved.

—*Ephesians 2:3-5*

Who was Jesus? How did He love? Jesus loved *so much* that He gave His life as the ultimate sacrifice so that our sins could be forgiven and we could have eternal life with God in heaven.

God delights in showing mercy. Consider what might happen if you forgave like Jesus. Pause for a moment and search your heart for any unforgiveness you've been holding onto. Ask God to reveal the names of people or situations where you need to practice forgiveness. Where can you extend grace and move from judgement to mercy, condemnation to encouragement, and from accusation to prayer and blessing?

As you practice walking in forgiveness, you will be amazed at the change it will bring to your life and relationships.

Invitation to Journey Deeper:

- Is there someone in your life you need to forgive? Release any resentment or bitterness towards them to God. Ask God to fill you with grace and mercy.
- Is there someone you need to forgive face-to-face? Ask the Lord for wisdom and discernment as you consider addressing this person.

For Further Reading: Matthew 7:1 and Isaiah 55:8-9

HE FIRST LOVED US

And so we know and rely on the love God has for us. God is love.
Whoever lives in love lives in God, and God in them.

—1 John 4:16

There have been so many times when I've had opportunities to love my enemies.

In business, I have been betrayed and had considerable losses from theft. Personally, I've been cheated on and suffered the devastating effects of physical and emotional assaults on my children. When these types of horrible things happen, there is usually not much opportunity to interact with the people involved, but there is always an ongoing opportunity to forgive, pray, and bless. As the Lord places these people on my heart who have done such damage, I simply release them through forgiveness and agree with His justice and mercy in prayer.

By praying for and blessing our enemies, we express the nature of the Father. We love God because He first loved us. We are to love our enemies and bless those who curse us.

> "So this is My command: Love each other deeply, as much as I have loved you. For the greatest love of all is a love that sacrifices all. And this great love is demonstrated when a person sacrifices his life for his friends. You show that you are My intimate friends when you obey all that I command you. I have never called you 'servants,' because a master doesn't confide in his servants, and servants don't always understand what the master is doing. But I call you My most intimate and cherished friends, for I reveal to you everything that I've heard from My Father. You didn't choose Me, but I've chosen and commissioned you to go into the world to bear fruit. And your fruit will last,

because whatever you ask of My Father, for My sake, He will give it to you! So this is my parting command: Love one another deeply!'"

—John 15:12-17, TPT

It is easy to love those who love us (at least typically), but Jesus loved the unlovable, including those who tortured and killed Him. He died for all and prayed for the Father to forgive them just before His death. The more we are in His presence, the more we can truly exhibit His exemplary love at a heart level. We cannot force ourselves to love others, especially our enemies, but we can submit ourselves and our ways to the Lord, choosing to love others because He first loved us. The more we abide in the vine, the more easily we can love God, love ourselves, and love our neighbours (even our enemies).

Invitation to Journey Deeper:

- Pause and think for a moment about what it means that God truly, deeply loves you. Journal your thoughts and then ask God to speak to you about His love for you.
- Are you living out of a place of God's love for you or from your own strength?
- Where is God calling you to experience or extend a greater sense of His love?

For Further Reading: 1 John 4:19 and Matthew 5:44

WITHOUT ME, YOU CAN DO NOTHING

That is why, for Christ's sake, I delight in weaknesses, in insults, in hardships, in persecutions, in difficulties. For when I am weak, then I am strong.

—2 Corinthians 12:10

God uses our faithfulness, in our weakness, to do mighty works by His Spirit. No one can adequately prepare to do this on their own... but His strength is made perfect in our weakness, and our humility (a result of surrender and dependence on God) provides access to His power. As we walk in faith and do the natural, God will do the supernatural.

Without the Holy Spirit, we can do nothing of eternal consequence. Our flesh is incapable of pleasing God on its own, which explains why Jesus said, apart from Him, we can do nothing. Anything cut off from God withers and dies. But by His grace, we are given the faith to see signs, wonders, and the miraculous.

My company recently faced an extremely difficult business situation that could have had a devastating impact. Our staff openly voiced their anxieties and fear. As we gathered in prayer, faith and boldness grew. The uncertainty and anxiety of our team turned to surrender. We continued to believe God's plan for us was for good. And if things didn't work out, we stood in confidence that God would have something else for us.

This means the one who plants is not anybody special, nor the one who waters, for God is the one who brings the supernatural growth.

—1 Corinthians 3:7, TPT

We committed to doing our part and would leave the outcome to Him and thank Him regardless of what it looked like in the natural world.

Defensive positioning turned to creativity as we leaned on the Lord. It brought our team together in unity more than ever before. New levels of trust, faith, and surrender have carried forward to this day because of this massive challenge. The result was better than we could have imagined!

It is not about us. It's all about Him and His limitless ability! Think about it; this is the message of the gospel! God is continually forming us into His image. Thank Him when things go according to plan. Thank Him when they don't. God is good and knows what we need and when we need it. Thank Him in all circumstances because He is using it. Nothing goes to waste with Him.

In order to bring heaven to earth as Jesus commanded, we must be filled with the strength of the Holy Spirit and stay connected to the body. He calls believers in Matthew 18:20 to pray together, "For where two or three gather in My name, there am I with them." Advancing the Kingdom is something we do together.

While many believers may never experience the fullness of God on this earth, His power is available to us here and now. I find my walk with the Lord is a continual process of operating in faith and prayer, doing my part in the natural world as God takes care of the supernatural. The pressure is off as God is in charge of how it all turns out. My job is to believe and agree. For me and every believer, obedience is success. In our weakness, we can trust Him to do mighty works!

Invitation to Journey Deeper:

- How have you experienced the Kingdom of God on earth?
- In what ways are you limiting your experience of God?
- What happens when you try to do things in your own strength? What could happen if you leaned fully on the Lord?

For Further Reading: Hebrews 11:6, John 15:5 and Ephesians 2:8-9

THE PATIENT JOURNEY TO FAITH

See, I have refined you, though not as silver; I have tested you in the furnace of affliction.

—Isaiah 48:10

I have seen the rescuing hand of God in dire circumstances. I have seen answers to prayers for deliverance and prayers for healing come quickly. However, seeing prayers answered is more often a process. Rarely do we pray and receive an instant, obvious answer. But... the waiting period produces character-building, life-transforming testimonies. Consider Abraham, Sarah, Hannah, Joseph, Moses, Job, and other heroes of the faith who contended for a breakthrough, some for decades. These men and women of God stood in faith despite what they could see with their natural eyes.

They are great examples for us to follow. I recommend taking a few minutes to read through Hebrews 11, which ends in verses 39-40 with the words, "These were all commended for their faith, yet none of them received what had been promised, since God had planned something better for us so that only together with us would they be made perfect." Even these heroes of the faith would not experience the fullness of God or all of His promises revealed in their lifetime.

Typically, an answer to prayer involves a series of breakthroughs where we strengthen and encourage one another on the journey. It requires vulnerability and openness in times of discouragement. Sowing seeds is a process, but know that a wonderful harvest will come!

And don't allow yourselves to be weary in planting good seeds, for the season of reaping the wonderful harvest you've planted is coming!

—Galatians 6:9, TPT

Even when we see a "sudden" answer to prayer, there has probably been an ongoing process behind the scenes. God has been at work, shaping our hearts, growing trust, and preparing the soil. The more time we spend with Him, the more our prayers will reflect His heart. God knows best. He uses the process of prayer and patience to refine us and mould us into His image.

Remember: Answered prayers don't always look how we might expect them to look. But God is faithful to answer. Though His answer may not be the one we want, God's ways are higher than our ways, and He is working all things together for the good of those who love Him.

Invitation to Journey Deeper:

- What prayer(s) are you waiting for God to answer?
- What prayer(s) have you already seen God answer? Did the wait feel long or short?
- Do you believe that God's answers are better than our requests and expectations? Why or why not?

For Further Reading: James 5:15 and Romans 8:28

GOING THROUGH THE VALLEY

For His anger lasts only a moment, but His favor lasts a lifetime;
weeping may stay for the night, but rejoicing comes in the morning.

—Psalm 30:5

We will all go through valleys, including the valley of the shadow of death. We will all experience the pain, frustration, and disappointment that comes when plans don't work out, a dream is unfulfilled, or something goes wrong, throwing our world into chaos. Whether it is the death of a loved one or a deep personal loss, we will all go through a valley at one point or another. The goal is not to build a house there. Keep moving. Pass through to the other side.

When hope is deferred, it is natural to feel disappointed. However, as believers, it is important not to allow our circumstances to dictate our emotions. On earth, our circumstances will never be perfect. We will need to give ourselves time and space to grieve and heal. Healthy grieving allows us to live healthy lives. However, we are not called to perpetual grief. Jesus said in Matthew 5:4, "Blessed are those who mourn, for they will be comforted." No matter what we are facing, we are promised comfort from the Father. He is trustworthy no matter how bad the situation we may be facing.

When facing disappointment, we can turn our faces to the Lord for comfort, new hope, and courage to keep going. If we do not, it opens the door to the enemy to plant seeds of discouragement and depression. The enemy's goal is to steal our hope and control our emotions. Satan discourages and deceives. He tells us there is no hope and that our story has no purpose. Jesus encourages and speaks truth over our lives. He speaks hope and victory over every circumstance.

Through Him, we can walk through the darkest valley with the hope of a good and beautiful future. If you are going through the valley of the shadow of death, if you are facing great disappointment, keep going. You will come through to the other side amazed by God's faithfulness. Weeping may come for the night, but joy comes in the morning.

Invitation to Journey Deeper:

- What valley is the Lord asking you to keep moving through?
- How can you show up for someone going through a valley?

For Further Reading: Psalm 30

KINGDOM COMMANDMENTS TO RELATIONSHIP

He answered, "'Love the Lord your God with all your heart and with all your soul and with all your strength and with all your mind'; and, 'Love your neighbor as yourself.'"

—Luke 10:27

In Luke 10:27, Jesus summarizes the Ten Commandments declared in Exodus 20:1-7 as follows: love God and love your neighbour as yourself. "Loving God" sums up the first five commandments and "loving your neighbour as yourself" sums up the last five commandments. Later, in John 13:34, Jesus further simplifies His command down to a single line, "Love one another as I have loved you, so you must love one another."

Paul defines love in his first letter to the Corinthians:

Love is patient, love is kind. It does not envy, it does not boast, it is not proud. It does not dishonor others, it is not self-seeking, it is not easily angered, it keeps no record of wrongs. Love does not delight in evil but rejoices with the truth. It always protects, always trusts, always hopes, always perseveres. Love never fails... And now these three remain: faith, hope and love. But the greatest of these is love.

—1 Corinthians 13:4-13

Love is choosing the highest good for all concerned. Love is beyond commitment; it is sacrifice. If we don't have love, we have nothing. We must learn to love people who are hurting and connect with their pain. As we feel the pain of others and love them, our light shines. When we love God, we naturally live a life of repentance and obedience. Love is everything in the Kingdom. He simply calls us to love others with His love. To be made into the likeness of Jesus is to love as He loves, which is a sign of real maturity. God's love...

>...is the only 100% secure attachment.
>...is supernatural and gives us compassion for those who need it most.
>...sets us free, releases hope, and changes us from the inside out.
>...shows us how to love ourselves and others.
>...is perfectly represented in the person of Jesus Christ.

Where there is love, there is no room for Satan. So, of course, Satan will try to separate, cause friction, and move our hearts towards condemnation and hate. But the choice is ours. We get to choose to partner with darkness or light, to extend mercy or judgement, to love or to hate.

Will you choose to love the way God loves? Or will you choose darkness?

Invitation to Journey Deeper:

- Draw a line down the centre of the page in your journal or sheet of paper. On one side, write down all of the things love is from 1 Corinthians 13:4-13. On the other side of the page, write down what love is *not*.
- Is there any area of your life where you have let darkness seep in? What would it look like if you chose love over hate in that area?
- Look up the Ten Commandments in Exodus 20:1-7, then read Jesus' command to love God and others in Luke 10:25-27 and John 13:34. How does this impact you and your understanding of Christianity?

For Further Reading: 1 Corinthians 13:2 and John 13:34

EXPRESSIONS OF GOD'S LOVE

But the fruit of the Spirit is love, joy, peace, forbearance, kindness, goodness, faithfulness, gentleness and self-control. Against such things there is no law.

—Galatians 5:22-23

The fruit of the Spirit represents the nature of God and the various expressions of His divine love. We experience this love, His perfect love, when we submit to His authority and connect with Him relationally. Paul mentions love first in the passage above for good reason: Everything good flows from love.

The presence of the fruit in our lives is an indicator of our relationship with Him. A friend of mine, Charles Zimmerman, describes it in this way:

The closer your relationship with Jesus, the more evident the fruit of the Spirit will be in your life. Picture the gauges in a car. When the gauges are low, ask Jesus, *What is keeping me from being filled with Your joy and peace?* While the specifics of what's getting in your way may vary, the answer to the gauges becoming full again will always be the same: Jesus.

The Holy Spirit working in and through us produces limitless fruit that looks like the character of Jesus. This fruit produced by the Holy Spirit within you is divine love in all its varied expressions: joy that overflows, peace that subdues, patience that endures, kindness in action, a life full of virtue, faith that prevails, gentleness of heart, and strength of spirit.

The more we draw close to God, the more we seek Him, the more we find Him. When we open our hearts to know God more and worship His name, it invites the Holy Spirit into our lives to mould and shape us to be more like Christ. The more we surrender to Him, the more our intimacy grows. The more we love the Word, the more our minds become renewed. Abiding becomes a lifestyle, and the fruit of the Spirit is a natural result.

You will seek Me and find Me when you seek Me with all your heart.

—Jeremiah 29:13

Invitation to Journey Deeper:

- Is there anything you have set above the qualities of the fruit of the Spirit? What are they?
- Are your gauges on empty or on full? What is keeping you from being filled with joy and peace from the Lord?

For Further Reading: Romans 14:17

KNOWN BY THEIR FRUIT

By their fruit you will recognize them. Do people pick grapes from thornbushes, or figs from thistles? Likewise, every good tree bears good fruit, but a bad tree bears bad fruit. A good tree cannot bear bad fruit, and a bad tree cannot bear good fruit.

—Matthew 7:16-18

The fruit produced by our lives is often a key indicator of our heart's position because the Bible teaches that a tree (or person) is known by its fruit. Punishment and performance bear religious and legalistic fruit. Love always manifests in good fruit that remains.

Rigid religious doctrines and sets of rules result from not having a relationship with Jesus. A religious spirit only produces orphans, whereas *relationship* produces sons and daughters. Encountering the Father's love does more to transform, heal, correct, and grow us than any set of rules!

The verses below describe the fruit our hearts can produce:

For where you have envy and selfish ambition, there you find disorder and every evil practice. But the wisdom that comes from heaven is first of all pure; then peace-loving, considerate, submissive, full of mercy and good fruit, impartial and sincere.

—James 3:16-17

The Spirit produces the *Kingdom fruit* of love, joy, peace, patience, kindness, goodness, faithfulness, gentleness, and self-control. Alternatively, earthly fruit (born of the flesh and legalism) opposes God and operates out of offence and judgement. We want to bear the best fruit out there. Soft and sweet, not hard and sour.

The fruit of my old life was a family in chaos and a business that was easily shaken. The more I abided, the more I changed—my life changed, my family changed, and my business changed. Despite circumstances and challenges, Galatians 5 fruit is now emerging everywhere!

The fruits of the Spirit are both outward and inward signs of the Holy Spirit at work within us. The more we abide in the Father's presence, the more our hearts become like Jesus and the more we reflect His nature. However, bearing fruit is not our primary aim as believers; it is abiding in Christ. Fruit is a natural by-product (not the goal) of abiding.[1] Bearing fruit simply shows that we are spiritually healthy and that our hearts are pointed and moving towards God. It is only by being connected to the vine and allowing His love to flow through us that we can love others. Let's continue to abide and bear good fruit!

Invitation to Journey Deeper:

- What kind of fruit are you bearing? If you aren't sure, ask God to show you.
- Who is an example of someone in your life bearing good fruit? What sets them apart?

For Further Reading: Galatians 5:22-23 and Romans 14:17

---

1. Mike Bickle, *Prayers to Strengthen Your Inner Man* (Kansas City: Forerunner Publishing, 2009), 10.

SACRIFICIAL LOVE

My command is this: Love each other as I have loved you.

—John 15:12

God's love is so much bigger than anything we can comprehend. True love is Christlike. It comes from a place of humility, which flows from a new heart or a born-again spirit united with Jesus. From this place, actions flow from God's love to become an expression of Jesus on earth, ultimately glorifying the Father. God so loved the world that He gave His Son as a sacrifice for us! Jesus endured the cross because of His love for us!

This love allows us to love our enemies and pray for those who persecute us. This love is sacrificial, and it is without expectation; it shows grace; it is volitional. We don't need to literally "feel" love to give or express it towards someone else. It is an act of will—not a feeling, but a choice. Small decisions regarding our daily actions can make a big impact on someone else's day and even their life. As we become more conformed to the image of Jesus, the more His love flows through us.

Everyone deserves to be loved because they are God's creation and created in His image. None of us are perfect, *and yet God loves us just as we are and loves us too much to leave us this way.* This is *agape* love, the highest form of love, which is sacrificial, unconditional, and selfless. Loving others with agape love increases our understanding of God's love for us. It is perfect; we are not. The more we love like God, the more others experience His love for them.

Agape love motivates Christians to serve and live amongst the poor, caring for the suffering, widows, and orphans. As the old story goes, fifteenth-century Moravians sold themselves into slavery to reach the lost as it was the only way to minister to the slave population. Countless martyrs have given their lives for the faith because of this love.

Do all Christians exhibit this love? No. This sort of sacrificial love is a fruit of the Spirit, which comes from intimacy with the Lord. When I was lukewarm, I did not comprehend love, although I thought I did. Now that I abide in Him, everything has changed. I have changed. I understand love differently.

This does not mean nonbelievers cannot love or do good works or have good motives. The world is capable of selfless love (there are selfless people all over the world in every culture). God is love and when we experience real love, we are experiencing God through people, believers or nonbelievers. However, with the fruit of the Spirit, the source of love and the motive of love are simply different. The more I seek God, the more the way I live my life reflects His love. As my heart changes, so does the way I see, treat, and care for others. By seeking the Source, my motive changes from a self-serving kind of love to a love that glorifies and honours God.

Invitation to Journey Deeper:

- Who do you know that displays Christ's love to others?
- When has someone sacrificed something to show *you* love?

For Further Reading: Matthew 5:44

MADE FOR CONNECTION

For just as each of us has one body with many members, and these members do not all have the same function, so in Christ we, though many, form one body, and each member belongs to all the others.

—Romans 12:4-5

As humans, we have a massive need for connection with God and with each other. This is because when God created humanity, He did so with the express purpose of creating *family*. Deeply embedded in our God-given DNA is our need for family and connection.

The 75-year long *Harvard Study on Adult Development* is the longest study on adult life ever done. It concludes that the level we feel connected to those around us is of primary importance in our measure of life satisfaction.[1] However, it is the quality, not the number of relationships, that matters. True connection not only makes us happier but also healthier.

In Genesis 2:18, God said, "It is not good for the man to be alone. I will make a helper suitable for him." Even the animals were not good enough for Adam. So God created Eve. Adam and Eve were the first family.

We serve a relational God who desires a relationship with us. He designed a world for us to experience that same kind of connection with other people. Though our earthly families will never satisfy the way God satisfies, they are a reminder of our dependence on Him. When we are young, we need our parents. When we are older, we will need our children. God made us to need one another. Scripture further reveals that no member of the body of Christ is certified to serve or function on their own. We are dependent on each other. Just as God has gifted me in certain ways, He has gifted you in other ways. We need others, and others need us. We are *all* dependent on God, our ultimate source and strength, while being interdependent with other believers.

We must be aware, the orphan wants a position and a title, while the son simply wants to serve and function in the role of a son. In humility, we place ourselves in service to the body of Christ and our function as God's children follows as we mature. All gifts and callings are equally important as we need one another to function as a body. We are needed!

We are one with Jesus and are to operate in oneness as a family. In fact, we are to go beyond fellowship. The Greek word *koinonia* refers to Christian fellowship, sharing everything in common and communion. Where I am weak, fellow believers on the journey with me are strong and lift me up and vice versa. Through my connection with other believers, I see a fuller view of Christ, merciful and just, patient and loving. As Proverbs 27:17 explains, "As iron sharpens iron, so one person sharpens another."

Invitation to Journey Deeper:

- How would you gauge your connection to the body of Christ? To your family? To God? What gifts do you have to offer your church on a practical or spiritual level?
- Are you familiar with koinonia? What would happen if believers came together in koinonia with their gifts to serve as one body?

For Further Reading: 1 Corinthians 12:12; 17 and Romans 12:5

---

1. "The Secret to Happiness," *Harvard Health Publishing: Harvard Medical School*, accessed January 28, 2022, https://www.health.harvard.edu/blog/the-secret-to-happiness-heres-some-advice-from-the-longest-running-study-on-happiness-2017100512543.

WHAT STOPS LOVE

For when you demonstrate the same love I have for you by loving one another, everyone will know that you're My true followers.

—John 13:35, TPT

Left unchecked and unhealed, hurts and traumas can open us up to demonic influence. They can stop us from receiving love from others and God. Knowing that God loves us with all of our weaknesses and failures allows us to love ourselves as He does.

On the other hand, many of us know how to love ourselves "too much" and choose a life of self-focus and gratification, which is the opposite of the commandment in Philippians 2:3, "Do nothing out of selfish ambition or vain conceit. Rather, in humility value others above yourselves."

All of this to say:

- If our hearts love the world, we cannot love God with all our hearts. (The "world" refers to self-idolatry, self-importance, and self-serving behaviour.)
- If our souls are not healed and are self-focused, we cannot love God with all of our souls.
- If our minds are not renewed, we cannot love God with all of our minds.
- If we don't love ourselves, we cannot love our neighbours.

We long to be fully known, fully accepted, and fully loved, just as we are. However, God is the ultimate connection that improves all other connections. To be loved by and to love God is how He designed us. God knows everything about us, will never disappoint us, and loves us unconditionally. He is the only one who can do this perfectly. Receiving this truth can literally heal our souls! The following prayer is by author and pastor Mike Bickle and is a guide to strengthening our inner man so we can truly love others the way God wants us to. I highly encourage you to spend some time with the Lord meditating on these words.

> *Father, pour out Your love into my inner man by the Holy Spirit that my heart may overflow in love back to you and to others (Rom 5:5). I also ask that You impart Your love for Jesus into my heart (John 17:26). I ask for grace to love God with all my heart, soul, mind and strength (Mark 12:30). Allow me to comprehend Jesus' love for me and to abide in it – stay connected to it (John 15:9). Let me see through Your eyes and love who you created me to be (Psalm 139:13-15).*[1]

Invitation to Journey Deeper:

Ask yourself the following questions as you reflect on the condition of your body, mind, and spirit.

- Do you love God or the world?
- Is your soul growing in health?
- Is your heart focusing more on God?
- Is your mind renewing?
- Are you learning to love yourself the way God loves you?

For Further Reading: Matthew 6:24

---

1. Mike Bickle, *Prayers to Strengthen Your Inner Man* (Kansas City: Forerunner Publishing, 2009), 10.

HEALTHY CONFRONTATION

There are individuals with high-conflict personalities who have the bad habit of "confronting " others with criticism, judgement, and manipulation. Often these people leave a wake of damage behind them. And sadly, these people are in the body of Christ. Sometimes they are even in church leadership. Engaging in conversation with such people is not fruitful. You have the choice not to take part or continue in unhealthy conversations. When in doubt, remember that healthy confrontation occurs between healthy people who have each other's best interest at heart.

With that in mind, be aware of your heart's position before correcting someone. If you are sharing out of an angry, annoyed, or bitter place, you probably need to keep quiet until you have dealt with the log in your own eye. If the person is in a fragile or vulnerable position, you want your words to be filled with God's peace and hope. It's possible the Lord is not asking you to say anything at all and just pray.

Remember: If you have a heart of love, encouragement, and compassion, and you have a green light from the Holy Spirit, share what the Lord has put on your heart. Love does something. Indifference does nothing. The opposite of love is indifference. Alternately, a heart of love welcomes correction and conviction. A heart of love is quick to repent and realign when an area of darkness or wrong thinking is exposed. Let's keep our hearts soft, loving, and open to whatever areas of growth the Lord may highlight through His Word or His church.

LOG IN
YOUR OWN EYE

We see most clearly in others what's most true in ourselves. The sin we call out in others might very well be our own sin that we are projecting on that person. As the saying goes, perception is projection. Matthew 7:1-3 provides us with a powerful warning about passing judgement and holding on to the wrongs done against us. If you are struggling with another person, you may be struggling with something within yourself. Before calling someone out, check your heart for your own sin that needs to be dealt with.

"Do not judge, or you too will be judged. For in the same way you judge others, you will be judged, and with the measure you use, it will be measured to you. Why do you look at the speck of sawdust in your brother's eye and pay no attention to the plank in your own eye?"
—Matthew 7:1-3

When giving correction, be real about how you have struggled yourself and be honest about your own mistakes. Do not swoop in with a "holier-than-thou" attitude. Be humble and kind. If you are going to someone in a vulnerable spot, you must show vulnerability.

I am so grateful for friends, mentors, intercessors, and pastors who have highlighted areas in my life or attitude that needed realignment or repentance. There was a time when I marched into my office filled with anxiety and strife over a certain negative circumstance. A friend had the courage to call me out and remind me that God had called me to walk in peace, not fear. I listened, felt convicted, repented, and received the gift of peace and forgiveness by God's grace. The rest of the day went much more smoothly.

Humility demands that I share transparently with my believing family what I am going through and feeling and will be there to walk people through their faith journey. I am open to correction and seek to offer correction to others when needed in love (not judgement). I do my best to offer course corrections when I have permission from the Holy Spirit. Whether they receive the correction is up to them; in the same way, I have a choice to be humble and respond to correction without offence.

LOVING CORRECTION

We are not called to pass judgement with an angry heart. To illustrate, rudely calling someone out for a superficial sin dealing with the non-essentials of the faith is probably coming from a critical place and certainly is not gentle or restorative! It is damaging and mean-spirited. However, a compassionate rebuke from a fellow believer dealing with an ungodly mindset, attitude, or behaviour is necessary for us all to grow in our faith and become more like Jesus. We all have blind spots. The wounds of a friend are faithful. Remember, it is God's kindness that leads to repentance!

There is a distinction between seeing sin in someone else's life and confronting it and having a critical, judgemental spirit. We are called to recognise and confront ungodly behaviour in other believers. Scripture encourages us to confront others according to a specific pattern outlined in Matthew 18 and Galatians 6 listed below:

"If your brother or sister sins, go and point out their fault, just between the two of you. If they listen to you, you have won them over. But if they will not listen, take one or two others along, so that 'every matter may be established by the testimony of two or three witnesses.' If they still refuse to listen, tell it to the church; and if they refuse to listen even to the church, treat them as you would a pagan or a tax collector."
—Matthew 18:15-17

Brothers and sisters, if someone is caught in a sin, you who live by the Spirit should restore that person gently. But watch yourselves, or you also may be tempted. Carry each other's burdens, and in this way you will fulfill the law of Christ. If anyone thinks they are something when they are not, they deceive themselves.
—Galatians 6:1-3

Note the line in Galatians that states we are called to restore that person gently. Paul does not command us to rebuke and leave that person hanging. Rather, we should rebuke and offer steps to restoration and healing.

Recently, I met a young executive who reminded me of myself at his age. His life was a mess, being slowly torn apart by selfishness and self-focus. I shared how I had been right where he was not long ago. I learnt the hard way where that road leads, but he didn't have to. Because I spoke in love and offered solutions for bringing healing to his life and family, he accepted my counsel. Today, he has new godly priorities ordering his life and is being mentored by godly older men. His life is back on track, and he is a new man. That is the fruit of godly correction!

WHO DO YOU THINK GOD IS?

For in Him all things were created: things in heaven and on earth,
visible and invisible, whether thrones or powers or rulers or authori-
ties; all things have been created through Him and for Him.

—Colossians 1:16

Twentieth-century English Bible teacher and author Arthur W. Pink
argues that:

> "The 'god' of the twentieth century no more resembles the Supreme
> Sovereign of Holy Writ then [sic] does the dim flickering of a candle
> the glory of the midday sun. The 'god' who is now talked about in the
> average pulpit, spoken of in the ordinary Sunday School, mentioned
> in much of the religious literature of the day, and preached in most of
> the so-called churches is the figment of human imagination, an inven-
> tion of maudlin sentimentality."[1]

How tragic such a view of God! And how wrong! To think Pink died in
1952, and yet this worldly view of God still stands today.

We tend to see God based on our own limited reasoning. We can see
Him as a wish-granter, or alternatively, the punishing parent. Your
culture, upbringing, and experience can all dangerously rewrite who
God is to fit your worldview. The god we project is a god we can
comprehend. *That* god does not exist.

The true God is so far beyond anything we could imagine! The original
scribes of the Bible refused to write God's name down or even say it
aloud because He is so holy. Instead, they wrote the Hebrew letters
YHWH (which we pronounce as "Yah-weh"), which means "I am."
That's how holy He is. Tragically, today, God's name is often only used
in vain.

Let's consider who we know God to be from Scripture. The list below only scratches the surface of the perfectly good, loving, powerful Creator. However brief and limiting this list is, it far outweighs the limited god most people have in their minds. Our God is:

- Omniscient (all-knowing)
- Omnipotent (all-powerful)
- Omnipresent (everywhere, all the time)
- Infinite
- Invincible
- Self-existing
- Without origin
- Never changing
- Self-sufficient, without need
- Perfectly wise
- Faithful
- Unchangingly true
- Infinitely good
- Kind and full of goodwill
- Infinitely just
- Merciful
- Compassionate and kind
- Gracious, inclined to spare the guilty
- Loving
- Holy
- Perfect
- Glorious, magnificent and beautiful

In our modern world and for the rest of time, let's be careful not to see God through our own limited understanding. That starts with how we see Him today!

Invitation to Journey Deeper:

- What characteristics would you add to this list?
- Why do you think the world (and even believers) limit who God is and what He can do?
- If you were to describe a twenty-first century idol or "god," what characteristics would you give it?

For Further Reading: Mark 10:18 and Psalm 145:9

---

1. Arthur W. Pink, "The God of the Twentieth Century," *Pristine Grace,* accessed January 7, 2021, https://www.pristinegrace.org/media.php?id=736.

CONNECTED TO OUR CREATOR

See what great love the Father has lavished on us, that we should be called children of God! And that is what we are! The reason the world does not know us is that it did not know Him.

—1 John 3:1

We all want a family who welcomes us with open arms no matter what. While our earthly families and communities may fill this need to a certain extent, truth be told, there is no substitute for a connection with our Creator. It is through this connection, the God-connection, that we are able to truly know, love, and accept others. A healthy connection with God allows us to connect in a healthy way with others.

God is looking for a family of sons and daughters. When we enter into a genuine relationship with God, He fulfils our core needs in the deepest way possible. If we look to people to meet this need instead of God, we will experience ongoing disappointment and hurt.

The God of the universe longs for relationships. God is a person. Jesus is a person. The Holy Spirit is a person. All three are one and yet divinely distinct and available for a unique one-on-one relationship with you and me. As soon as we grasp this profound truth, our lives will never be the same.

As it says in Matthew 5:8, "Blessed are the pure in heart, for they will see God." We can see Jesus in every relationship if we receive His revelation. Ask Him to open the eyes of your heart to see Him in every situation you're facing, good or bad. Ask Him to show you how He is woven through the fabric of creation.

Invitation to Journey Deeper:

- What area of your life are you letting people fulfill needs only God can truly satisfy?
- Is God a part of all aspects of your life? What part of your life do you need to invite God into?

For Further Reading: Ephesians 1:5

Part Four

Suffering for the Believer

And we know that in all things God works for the good of those
who love Him, who have been called according to His purpose.

—Romans 8:28

To suffer means to submit to or be forced to endure death, pain, or distress. There are various degrees of suffering we will all experience in life. There is mild suffering like learning a skill, minor discomforts and inconveniences, etc. There is the pain of physical suffering that comes with injury, illness, and the effects of aging. And there is internal, emotional suffering that comes with the loss of a loved one, a dream, or a desired outcome.

Suffering and pain are inevitable. It is part of the common human experience, something everyone can relate to on some level. Jesus suffered in every degree, except for the suffering that resulted from sin, as He was sinless. He toiled as a carpenter and experienced the aches, pains, loss, and grief that accompany life on earth. He suffered incredible pain on the cross, even feeling abandoned (forsaken) by God in the physical and emotional torment that came with being crucified. The greatest expression of love is sacrificial—Jesus gave His life for you and me. *Jesus suffered to redeem us.*

The key foundation for our journey in life is knowing God's never-changing character. God is always kind, always just, always faithful, always patient, always good, always merciful, and His grace is always sufficient. We are always to lean back on the character of God, our perfect Father, as our rock in times of suffering!

God offers comfort in our suffering, which is what I experienced in the aftermath of my daughter's death. Losing a child is something no parent should go through, but God showed up in a big way when it happened to me. The peace and joy I felt after Abbe's murder were not of this world. I didn't expect to experience these emotions just hours after the murder of my daughter, and the fact that I did caused many to resent and judge me. The truth is, I was processing a tremendous loss and suffering a great deal, but I wasn't doing it alone. I had a history of abiding in God, and by His grace, He released me from the over-whelming loss of Abbe. I knew she was safely home, and He was by my side no matter what might lie ahead.

Asher Intrater, prolific author and founder of Revive Israel Ministries, describes suffering in the believer's life beautifully:

> *We all recoil at the thought of suffering. Suffering itself is NOT a good thing in and of itself. However, when one suffers in a godly way, there is an emotional and spiritual intimacy with Yeshua. He suffered. You are sharing part of that experience with Him. It is the shared experience that is beautiful. Intimacy in the midst of suffering is precious. It is worth the price.*[1]

In this section, I want to encourage you to lean on the Father as your source of strength, comfort, peace, and joy in whatever circumstance you may be facing. Not all suffering looks the same. We all come into this world self-focused, needing redirection and a Saviour to redeem us.

Through our trials, discipline, correction, training, submission, and willingness to die to self, God turns our hearts towards Him and makes us more like Him. If we allow Him, God will take our suffering and use it for His glory. Patient endurance or long-suffering result in maturity. Whether our suffering results from our own sin and unwise choices or the choices of others, God can use it to transform us into the likeness of Jesus.

No matter what you are going through or what you have already been through, know that God is always good. God redeems and restores! He will never leave you nor forsake you. He is our refuge and our strength, our greatest comfort in times of trouble. He turns our ashes into beauty.

---

1. Asher Intrater, "The Fellowship of His Suffering," *RITG*, accessed December 10, 2021, https://www.ritg.org/post/the-fellowship-of-his-suffering.

SOVEREIGNTY OF GOD

For in Him all things were created: things in heaven and on earth, visible and invisible, whether thrones or powers or rulers or authorities; all things have been created through Him and for Him. He is before all things, and in Him all things hold together.

—Colossians 1:16-17

Scripture affirms again and again that God is good. In fact, *only* God is good. So, if God is good, why do we suffer?

The answer is simple. *Man's sin.* Even though God is fully in charge, He honours our free will. He allows us to reap the consequences, good or bad, of our actions. And sometimes, we reap the consequences, good or bad, of others' actions. We may not receive what appears to be just or right in this life, but in the end, God's justice is perfect and will prevail. No matter how far we veer off the path or fail, our sovereign, all-powerful God, will redeem us if we submit everything to Him.

God made the earth and the entire universe function according to His Word and His ways. This system allows humanity to demonstrate the dominion of God on earth. God created all and, therefore, everything is subject to Him. He has eternity in mind. No matter what it looks like on earth, you can trust in His eternal plan.

And through His creative inspiration this Living Expression made all things, for nothing has existence apart from Him!

—John 1:3, TPT

Nothing comes your way that God does not allow. He is completely sovereign and in charge, and nothing can stop His plan for redemption. Although He makes all things work for our good, not everything we experience is God's idea. God has chosen not to control every event or outcome of our lives (though He certainly could!) because He values human agency. The gift of freedom was an act of love. Our freedom to choose how we behave makes authentic relationships possible. The potential for evil and sin exists because of free choice. In addition, Satan needs legal access before God will allow him to act, as in the book of Job.

The fall of man in the Garden of Eden set our ship terribly off course, and we've been dealing with the deadly, tragic consequences ever since. Out of His utmost mercy, God sent His Son to set our ship back on course... but the storm still rages. He has ultimately won the war, but we all have battles to face until Jesus returns or He calls us home. In the meantime, the power of the Holy Spirit will help us navigate life in a system broken by man's rebellion and inhabited by a demonic, evil spirit realm at odds with God.

God's ways are always right. They may not make sense to us. They may be mysterious, difficult, and even painful. But they are right, and they are, ultimately, good.

Invitation to Journey Deeper:

- Do you struggle to make sense of God's ways? Why or why not?
- How have you seen God turn a difficult situation or experience into something good?

For Further Reading: Mark 10:8 and Job 1:12

THE REDEEMER OF ALL

Very truly I tell you, you will weep and mourn while the world rejoices. You will grieve, but your grief will turn to joy.

—John 16:20

As a loving Father, God equips us with His grace to overcome whatever this world throws our way. God not only empathises and relates to our pain, but He also does something about it. Whether what we experience results from our own missteps or those of others, God is there with us when we need Him most.

The suffering we feel for a loved one in turmoil can be far greater than personal suffering, as any parent will attest. As a father, I suffered in the wake of the immense pain that both of my daughters faced in their youth. Both Abbe and Bryn lost their childhoods, suffering physical, sexual, and emotional abuse. This led to mental illness, drug addiction, sexual confusion, and suicide attempts for both my girls. For Abbe, it led to a life on the streets that ended in her violent murder.

I felt intense helplessness as Abbe plunged further and further into darkness. I felt her pain and disconnection from our family. I felt sadness, regret, shame, anger, disbelief, and sorrow. I grieved the loss of so many years of our relationship when she was in rehab. There were times of anguish where we held firm to ultimatums resulting in Abbe choosing homelessness over help. I was devastated seeing her wrists stitched up following one of her suicide attempts.

As I reflected on my many bad choices and parenting mistakes, there was suffering. I deeply regretted unknowingly placing Abbe and Bryn in harm's way. I regretted breaking up and destabilising our family through divorces. I was saddened and upset by my lack of discernment as a father and protector.

These were areas I needed God's healing. Receiving God's forgiveness and forgiving others allowed my healing process to begin in the midst of suffering. Continuing to trust God and hold onto His promises in the mystery, leaning on biblical truths and depending on His goodness, strengthened me and brought hope. Learning to share openly and honestly with close friends and God, receiving healing, and allowing Jesus into my memories, disappointment, and hurt, diffused shame and created connection and intimacy. I held on to the truth that He redeems the lost, brings to life what is dead, and heals the broken. Today, I have seen Him redeem my life and my family in powerful ways. We are all different people because of His miracle-working power in the aftermath of great tragedy.

No matter what you face, I encourage you to do the same. Hold on to the truth that God redeems what is lost, brings to life what is dead, and heals what is broken.

Invitation to Journey Deeper:

- How has suffering impacted you or your relationship with God?
- In what seasons has your faith grown the most—in times of comfort or hardship?
- What promise is God asking you to hold on to?

For Further Reading: 2 Corinthians 1:3-4, John 16:20, Hebrews 13:5, Psalm 46:1 and Isaiah 61:3

EMBRACING THE MYSTERY

I remain confident of this: I will see the goodness of the Lord in the land of the living.

—Psalm 27:13

God is never surprised.

He will never leave you.

He will never forsake you.

And He is *always* good.

His grace is more than sufficient.

We will each face circumstances we may never understand until we are with God in heaven. Times of mystery require faith. These moments challenge us to pray God's will is done on earth as it is in heaven. This understanding provides us with peace and great assurance. This, and knowing that God is always good, allows us to walk through life on earth with faith and hope that God will turn everything around for our good and His glory.

Life is full of big and small challenges, which can be incredibly overwhelming. But God tells us those aren't our burdens to carry! Matthew 6:26-34 reminds us that if God cares for the birds of the air, then surely He will care for us.

Opportunities to trust God in the unknown, through seasons of pain and confusion, are what faith and trust are all about. These moments test our character and develop maturity in Christ. When we rely on God for our daily portion, it creates a dependence on Him. It also invites us to share with Jesus in His suffering on the cross. The victor's crown is the reward for those who successfully reach the end, still trusting and believing that God is good.

Everyone who competes in the games goes into strict training. They do it to get a crown that will not last, but we do it to get a crown that will last forever.

—1 Corinthians 9:25

Trials, tribulations, and suffering are guaranteed, but our good and compassionate Creator of the universe is with us. He understands our suffering. Although we only see in part, God's view is eternal and far beyond our ability to comprehend, so we must learn to let go and trust Him.

Invitation to Journey Deeper:

- What struggles or worries do you carry with you? What would it look like if you gave those concerns over to God?
- How can you encourage or point others to Jesus in seasons of struggle?

For Further Reading: Matthew 6:33-34

THE FELLOWSHIP OF SUFFERING

But we have this treasure in jars of clay to show that this all-surpassing power is from God and not from us. We are hard pressed on every side, but not crushed; perplexed, but not in despair; persecuted, but not abandoned; struck down, but not destroyed. We always carry around in our body the death of Jesus, so that the life of Jesus may also be revealed in our body... So then, death is at work in us, but life is at work in you.

—2 *Corinthians* 4:7-12

The Corinthians reading these words would have understood these jars to be basic, everyday items. Different jars served different purposes. Fragile and imperfect jars on the outside did not always reflect the value of the contents inside. Paul compares believers to these jars. We are the created clay vessels of the Master Potter, designed to carry His presence through the death and resurrection of Christ.

God sent His one and only Son as a sacrifice for all so that anyone who believes would be free to live with Him in eternity. Jesus' crucifixion was so awful, we will never understand the physical, mental, and emotional anguish He went through. Jesus even cried out to God from the cross in immense pain. Because of the gift of the cross, we no longer have to fear death. However, this does not mean our lives will be free from sorrow and suffering. Following Jesus challenges the world's ways. It shines a light on the darkness, which invites persecution. In other words, our fragile clay bodies may get an extra crack or two on the journey, but we will make it to eternity safe and sound. Through the persecution and suffering we will experience as believers, we get to share in Jesus' sufferings. This forges deep intimacy with fellow believers and with Jesus and is known as the "fellowship of His suffering."[1] In this sense, suffering is a blessing, even when it doesn't feel like it. In fact,

His apostles rejoiced that they had been found worthy to suffer for His name.

> *In my life or in my death, Christ will be magnified in me. My true life is the Anointed One, and dying means gaining more of Him.*
>
> *—Philippians 1:21, TPT*

Paul experienced joy and gave thanks in every circumstance, no matter how brutal. He gave his life fully to the Lord. Paul loved people and wanted to share the gospel, but he also wanted to be liberated from his body to be fully joined with Christ. He lived without fear of death. Today, His words invite us to do the same. And because of our imperfections, cracks, and the places where God has bound us back together through the trials and tribulations of life, the light of what's inside can shine through. Our light shines in the darkness, and it will not be overcome.

Invitation to Journey Deeper:

- Do you view suffering as a blessing or curse? Why?
- How does your view of suffering change when you read 2 Corinthians 4:7-12?

For Further Reading: Isaiah 64:8, John 1:5; 3:16, Matthew 27:46 and Acts 5:41

---

1. Asher Intrater, "The Fellowship of His Suffering," *RITG*, accessed December 10, 2021, https://www.ritg.org/post/the-fellowship-of-his-suffering.

REFINING FIRE

He will sit as a refiner and purifier of silver; He will purify the Levites and refine them like gold and silver. Then the Lord will have men who will bring offerings in righteousness.

—*Malachi* 3:3

Then He said to them all: "Whoever wants to be My disciple must deny themselves and take up their cross daily and follow Me."

—*Luke* 9:23

There is much to understand and much we may never fully understand about human suffering. Many nonbelievers and believers alike ask questions such as:

- Why do people suffer?
- Why do bad things happen to good people?
- Why do we feel pain?
- Why does evil exist?
- Why doesn't God end suffering in the world (hunger, poverty, disease, homelessness, etc.)?

The list is endless, and so are the explanations given to answer these questions. Thankfully, Scripture gives us a framework to understand Christian suffering through the eyes of God.

First, some suffering is of our own making or the making of others. Galatians 6:7-8 states that we will reap what we sow. God gave us dominion over the earth. He choses to intervene in His creation *through* us. We were created to create solutions to any problem we create, with His help. Sometimes, we blame God for evil that goes unchallenged or unchecked. Could it be that He is waiting for us to bring His truth and light to deception and darkness?

Second, some suffering is from Satan. In the book of Job, we see Satan attack a man of God on all fronts. In one day, Job loses his animals, his staff, and his children. His entire life turns upside down. Satan challenges God in Job 2:5, saying, "But now stretch out your hand and strike his flesh and bones, and he will surely curse you to your face." Even Job's wife in verse 9 says to "Curse God and die!" for his misery. And yet Job never backs down. He trusts in the almighty God, knowing that God is still at work in his suffering.

I relate a lot to Job, more than I would like to sometimes. And I am sure you've gone through seasons of loss like he did, too. If there is anything we can all agree on, it's the pain that accompanies adversity. But I can assure you, God will meet you in the midst of your suffering! Regardless of the source of our suffering, if we stick with Him through it, He will provide the grace to endure.

Finally, some suffering comes from God as He forms us into the image of His Son.

> *See, I have refined you, though not as silver; I have tested you in the furnace of affliction.*
>
> —Isaiah 48:10

God will allow or cause delay, disappointment, discouragement, and other difficult circumstances to shape us, bring us to the end of ourselves, and develop greater dependence on Him. These circumstances allow us to learn the discipline of praising the Lord and trusting Him through testing and are occasionally the direct answer to our prayers for God to refine us.

The process of discipleship means to undergo *discipline*, to take up our cross as a part of our training to become like Jesus. The Lord disciplines those He loves. We must learn to submit to His discipline and endure in His strength.

At the end of the day, it doesn't matter if these types of tests are attacks from Satan or from the Lord, He is using everything for our good. As self-pity or self-reliance surface, I come face-to-face with my weakness and need to depend on Him.

God was answering my prayers and, although painful, discouraging or downright frustrating on my end, God was maturing me in a new way. Now, I regularly pray for God to refine me in His fire and to have His way in my life.

Through it all, I am learning humility and obedience. I am learning to encourage myself in the Lord. I am learning thankfulness, even when I don't like my circumstances.[1] I am growing in courage and perseverance. I know the trials of our faith cause our roots to go deep. As 1 Peter 1:7 states, "These have come so that the proven genuineness of your faith—of greater worth than gold, which perishes even though refined by fire—may result in praise, glory and honour when Jesus Christ is revealed."

Philippians 3:10 says, "I want to know Christ—yes, to know the power of His resurrection and participation in His sufferings, becoming like Him in His death." This verse describes three ways we are made into Christ's image. First, to know Him. Second, to know the power that raised Him from the dead, and third, to know Him in his suffering. So, we are called to be conformed to Christ by coming together with Him in suffering.[2]

God does not delight in our suffering, but rather, He delights in our obedience. Just as Jesus learnt to listen and obey through His suffering, He invites us to the freedom that comes from dependence on Him. Suffering is part of the sanctification process where we die to ourselves to become increasingly more Christlike. He wants the fullness of His creation to be revealed. God is good!

> When God gets us alone through suffering, heartbreak, temptation, disappointment, sickness, or by thwarted desires, a broken friendship,

or a new friendship—when He gets us absolutely alone, and we are totally speechless, unable to ask even one question, then He begins to teach us.

—Oswald Chambers[3]

Invitation to Journey Deeper:

- What does it mean to deny yourself, take up your cross, and follow Jesus?
- In what ways have you suffered or died to yourself in the process of becoming more Christlike?
- What areas of your life do you feel God pruning right now?

For Further Reading: Hebrews 5:8 and Luke 9:23

---

1. Read Habakkuk 3:17-19 to discover the power of a thankful heart and the key to victory!
2. Asher Intrater, "The Fellowship of His Suffering," *RITG*, accessed December 10, 2021, https://www.ritg.org/post/the-fellowship-of-his-suffering.
3. Oswald Chambers, "Have You Ever Been Alone with God?" *My Utmost for His Highest*, accessed February, 19, 2022, https://utmost.org/have-you-ever-been-alone-with-god-2/.

SUFFERING

There are many types of suffering. Paul tells the church at Corinth in 2 Corinthians 4:8, "We are hard pressed on every side, but not crushed; perplexed, but not in despair." He acknowledges there are many types of suffering, not just one. Mental, emotional, physical, spiritual — we will experience them all. When we deny ourselves, we suffer. Take fasting, for example: We deny ourselves by willingly removing food, media, or anything else that our flesh depends on for comfort, pleasure, or distraction to help us focus on God as our comforter.

SUFFERING PREPARES US TO DO KINGDOM WORK

As we experience different struggles, God gives us tools to minister to those who will benefit from our experiences. In 2 Corinthians 1:3-4, it states, "Praise be to the God and Father of our Lord Jesus Christ, the Father of compassion and the God of all comfort, who comforts us in all our troubles, so that we can comfort those in any trouble with the comfort we ourselves receive from God." When the source of our comfort is God, our suffering has a purpose. Similarly, 1 Peter 4:1 explains, "Therefore, since Christ suffered in His body, arm yourselves also with the same attitude, because whoever suffers in the body is done with sin." Without experiencing our own suffering, how could we comfort someone else in need? When we trust God, knowing He is producing a good work in us, we can suffer with the same attitude as Christ.

GOD DOES NOT WANT US TO SUFFER ALONE

In his letter to the Galatians, Paul tells the believers in Galatians 6:2 to "Carry each other's burdens, and in this way, you will fulfill the law of Christ." We are to bear the weight of suffering together as the church, not alone. This requires openness and vulnerability. When there is a need, it is the church's job to meet it. As believers, if someone is struggling, we must surround our brothers and sisters to support and cover them. God is communal, and He designed the church and His people to reflect His relational nature.

SUFFERING INVITES US TO GLORY

Suffering is temporary and calls us back to God. 2 Corinthians 4:17-18 states, "For our light and momentary troubles are achieving for us an eternal glory that far outweighs them all. So we fix our eyes not on what is seen, but on what is unseen, since what is seen is temporary, but what is unseen is eternal." It is essential to view suffering from an eternal perspective. In this light, the rewards of suffering far outweigh the costs. As Christ's suffering became our reward, our own suffering brings us closer to the glory of the cross. We are told to deny ourselves and bear our cross. The cross brings death to self. Death proceeds resurrection life through daily choices to follow Christ. These small ongoing daily changes lead to abundant life, increasing glory and Christlikeness.

THE PATH TO MATURITY

The Lord is good to all; He has compassion on all He has made.

—Psalm 145:9

God has our eternal well-being in mind and knows what is best for us. Be open to the crushing. The crushing leads to blessing. Crushing produces new wine, and in new wine, there is new life and great freedom. The result is maturity, character, patient perseverance (long-suffering), and unshakeable hope to run the race of our faith.

The "gift" (I still cringe a bit using this word, but I know it is the truth) of suffering produces eternal fruit. It changed my perspective and forever changed my life with the Lord. Suffering accelerates the ongoing process of dying to self like nothing else could. As Scripture says in John 12:24, "Very truly I tell you, unless a kernel of wheat falls to the ground and dies, it remains only a single seed. But if it dies, it produces many seeds." The greater the emptying of self, the greater the Christlikeness, the greater the fruit, the greater the glory. When we suffer, Jesus mourns with us. Draw near to Him, and He will draw near to you.

When I truly gave my life to God, I had increasingly less and less in common with the world. The result was even *more* suffering as my relationships with family and friends changed. Some of those closest to me felt I had become a fanatic. They said I was not the same person I was before... and they were right. Losing these relationships was painful and left me in a lonely place. However, realising these people preferred the old version of me became a clear indicator of the growth happening within me.

Though I didn't realise it, God was deeply forming me through the trials. Though I grieved my flesh's death, it was critical to my transformation in Christ. Now I look to the Lord to fill my deepest longings and needs, and He has blessed me with many life-giving relationships within the body of Christ. He will do the same for you!

There is blessing on the other side of the crushing. Testing and trials produce endurance, but we can count it all joy because of His tender compassion. God is good, and His love endures. Faith and joy come as we abide in His presence. And I can assure you, there is no sweeter reward than the comfort of the Lord's embrace as He takes on every burden we carry.

Invitation to Journey Deeper:

- What have you grieved from your former life? (i.e., relationships, lifestyle, hobbies, etc.)
- Who have you seen experience great suffering for the sake of the cross? What have you learnt from his/her story?
- How have you experienced the Lord's compassion in your suffering?

For Further Reading: James 1:2-4; 4:8

REAPING AND SOWING

Do not be deceived: God cannot be mocked. A man reaps what he sows. Whoever sows to please their flesh, from the flesh will reap destruction; whoever sows to please the Spirit, from the Spirit will reap eternal life.

—Galatians 6:7-8

God made the world in such a way that we reap what we sow. Our choices have consequences that ripple down. Choices rooted in selfishness and pride, or alternately selflessness and love, affect future generations. Our choices ultimately make up the inheritance we give to our children and future generations, so we must choose wisely.

There is an old story tracing the legacies of two family lines. The first line descends from Jonathan Edwards, a Puritan Preacher in the eighteenth century. Jonathan (a graduate of Yale and Princeton and one of the most respected preachers of his day) and his wife Sarah dedicated their lives to making sure their children knew God and served Him. Over the next 150 years, his legacy includes "1 U.S. vice-president, 1 dean of a law school, 1 dean of a medical school, 3 U.S. senators, 3 governors, 3 mayors, 13 college presidents, 30 judges, 60 doctors, 65 professors, 75 military officers, 80 public office holders, 100 lawyers, 100 clergymen, and 285 college graduates."[1]

Compare this legacy to that of Jonathan Edwards' contemporary, Max Jukes. Max, a New York native with a shady past (his wife also had a similar background), was not interested in teaching his children anything to do with a godly lifestyle. In contrast to Edwards, Jukes' descendants included "7 murderers, 60 thieves, 190 prostitutes, 150 other convicts, 310 paupers, and 440 who were physically wrecked by addiction to alcohol. Of the 1,200 descendants that were studied, 300 died prematurely."[2]

...According to the Bible, the problem is not the strength or kindness of God. The problem is the agenda of the human race. We pursue the wrong priority.

—Max Lucado[3]

Unrepented sin carries down through the ages, affecting generation after generation and even the earth itself. Creation carries scars from men's selfishness and pride, just as we all do. Crisis and chaos are the fruit of following the wrong gods (ourselves or idols). Our God is a just God. He cannot ignore sin. Like any good Father, God disciplines those He loves. How we respond to His discipline dictates which way we will go. The choices you make today affect more than just you. Your actions will trickle down through future generations as blessings or curses.

Invitation to Journey Deeper:

- How is the Holy Spirit inviting you to engage in the redemption of your family legacy?
- In what ways is the Father drawing you back to Himself?
- How can you establish roots of selflessness and love in your life?

For Further Reading: Proverbs 13:22

---

1. Larry Ballard, "Multigenerational Legacies–The Story of Jonathan Edwards," *Family Ministries*: Youth With a Mission, accessed February 14 2021, https://www.ywam-fmi.org/news/multigenerational-legacies-the-story-of-jonathan-edwards/.
2. Ibid.
3. James Lau, "Nothing comes our way without His permission and presence by Max Lucado," *My Inward Journey*, accessed February 19, 2022, https://jameslau88.com/2020/05/09/nothing-comes-our-way-without-his-permission-and-presence-by-max-lucado/.

OUR HEART'S DESIRE

So above all, guard the affections of your heart, for they affect all that you are. Pay attention to the welfare of your innermost being, for from there flows the wellspring of life.

—Proverbs 4:23, TPT

The desires of our hearts will become manifest on earth through the choices we make and the lifestyle we lead. Before submitting to Christ, I lacked wisdom and discernment. I was inconsistent and impulsive in the choices I made. I moved too quickly to stop and learn from my mistakes. My desire to be viewed as a strong provider took precedence over my identity as a beloved son of God. This expressed itself in compromise and choosing what I thought was best over what was God's best. I had external success, but my life and family were completely void of real peace, security, and the awareness of the unconditional love of God.

Unresolved heart issues (wounds, a mediocre faith-life, rebellion, etc.) left me bound and blinded. This blindness manifested into making poor parenting, business, and life decisions. Subconsciously, this path seemed like a much easier and safer route than opening myself up to working through the unresolved pain of my youth, failed marriages, and other traumas.

However, after submitting my life to Jesus and focusing on Him and who I was to Him, my desires changed. God became my aim and family my top priority. That said, even though I had made new decisions that put my family first, I was still reaping the consequences of the old seeds I had sown. It would take time for the new seeds to take root and grow.

Eventually, by the grace of God, this season would produce an incredible harvest. I now know my house must be in order before anything else. Transformed hearts transform lives, which transforms families, which changes society and shifts world history.

> *Let us not become weary in doing good, for at the proper time we will reap a harvest if we do not give up.*
>
> —*Galatians 6:9*

We don't always know the level of spiritual opposition contributing to our issues. Even if you are doing everything "right" (which was not happening in my case), everyone still faces the fire of trials and tribulations in their journey. These painful and dark struggles are used to prepare us for what the Lord has in store so that we will responsibly steward the weight of what God will ask us to do (with His strength!). The choices we make every day determine what sort of crop we will harvest in due season.

Invitation to Journey Deeper:

- What harvest are you reaping today? Consider your work, personal, home, and spiritual life. How can you invest in each of these areas *now* for a future harvest?
- What is your heart's desire? Where do you spend your time and energy? Does your life reflect the world's desires or God's desires?

For Further Reading: 1 Samuel 16:7

A HEART AFTER GOD

God, I invite Your searching gaze into my heart. Examine me through and through; find out everything that may be hidden within me. Put me to the test and sift through all my anxious cares.

—Psalm 139:23, TPT

Choosing to worship God, no matter your circumstance, will reap incredible (and eternal) rewards. When Job's children died, he continued to worship God. The same happened with David after his son died; he worshipped the Lord. Following their example, I chose to make Abbe's funeral in May 2018 an opportunity to worship and glorify God.

Choosing to worship does not minimise the extreme pain that accompanies the loss of a loved one. If you are going through any type of loss right now, I grieve with you. I understand. I also encourage you to worship your Father in heaven. No matter how good or bad the situation you're in may be, worship is always the right response! God is always worthy of our praise.

At the same time we lost Abbe, I also experienced many other losses. My marriage was over. My brother pushed my sister and me away through his lifestyle choices and unhealed pain from our childhood trauma... but my relationships with Bryn, my sister, Barb, and my mother came around in an undeniably powerful, supernatural way. The Holy Spirit moved powerfully to restore and transform the very thing I had been so afraid to focus on before: my family. Choosing to hold on to the love of God, although challenging, proved incredibly fruitful.

The restoration of my heart led me to pursue new connections with those that I loved as He brought me into a greater level of intimacy with Him. It was a type of love and connection I had never known. He taught me to re-establish healthy boundaries and reconstruct my entire life according to His plans. One small step at a time, my life was (and continues to be) totally transformed, and the fruit of my relationship reflected the drastic change.

Though the loss of my former life was difficult at first, I discovered there is no greater joy than seeking God's heart. It far outweighs any achievements or experiences I've had in this life because He is the embodiment of perfect love. His love is for me, and it is for you, too. It is not our performance or perfection that earns His love, but His love for us that makes our joy complete. We receive His joy as a fruit of the Spirit and the joy of the Lord is our strength!

Invitation to Journey Deeper:

- Who or what is the foundation of your life?
- When times are hard, is your foundation firm? Why or why not?
- How have you experienced the joy of the Lord?

For Further Reading: Job 1, 2 Samuel 12 and John 15:11

TRANSFORMATION

Severe pressures can reveal what hides inside our hearts. Proverbs 27:21-22 expresses the other side of the coin: *"The crucible for silver and the furnace for gold, but people are tested by their praise. Though you grind a fool in a mortar, grinding them like grain with a pestle, you will not remove their folly from them."* God's light shining on darkness in our lives gives us an opportunity to walk into healing and deliverance. Suffering for the believer...

...allows our character to shine through.	...brings us to the end of ourselves.
...refines and purges us of the things of this world.	...matures us.
...exposes the depth of our hearts and what is hidden inside.	...makes us aware of our weaknesses, brokenness, emotions, and need for God.
...makes us more dependent on God.	...produces humility.
...leads to greater surrender.	...brings us closer to God.

...increases our compassion and mercy for others.	...deepens our need, relationship, and connection with the body of Christ.
...awakens us to His presence, His Word, and His voice.	...strengthens and shapes us (the process of sanctification).
..shifts our focus from the things of the world to the things above.	...when met with perseverance, produces a tender heart.
..forms character.	...prepares us for what is ahead.

FOR OUR GOOD

Israel, put your hope in the Lord, for with the Lord is unfailing love and with Him is full redemption.

—Psalm 130:7

Through all things, we can trust that God's ways are always good and full of hope. I have suffered well, and I have suffered poorly. As I look back on my life, when my focus was on myself, I suffered unto death. My sense of entitlement and self-pity led to anxiety, depression, and discouragement. When I focused on Him and rested in His presence, I suffered unto life. Abiding produces the fruits of the Spirit, which are not dependent on circumstances.

The Bible is very clear: We are to deny ourselves, take up our crosses, present ourselves as living sacrifices and not love our lives unto death. If this is our heart's position, we can endure whatever comes our way and come out stronger, empowered by grace. When we trust God, we relinquish the need to control our circumstances. We are not our own. We are bought at a price.

Suffering met with self-pity will not produce good fruit. In fact, it will defile you and those around you. Suffering met with a soft, teachable heart results in remarkable growth. Nothing has transformed me more than suffering. While God does not delight in our suffering, He does use it to point out our blind spots and areas that are not yet surrendered to Him.

Pain has a way of intensifying our focus. The question is, will you put your focus on God or on the struggle you are facing? Although it can be difficult, and sometimes I still fail, I choose to glorify God. When I put my focus on Him, the peace, joy, and presence of God wash over me, and I am renewed.

Our challenges test and form us in preparation for what God has in store for us. God's ways are higher than our own. We must allow His good and perfect purposes to be fulfilled.

The good news is that God can handle me at my best and at my worst (and everywhere in between). He understands the depth of our struggles and why choosing Him is not always easy. In Matthew 27:46, Jesus cried out from the cross, "My God, My God, why have You forsaken Me?" Yes, even Jesus felt forgotten and alone on the cross. We share in His suffering, and He shares in ours. But God doesn't change. He is always with us, always there to comfort and bring peace as He works to fulfil His purposes.

Invitation to Journey Deeper:

- Are you suffering well, or are you suffering poorly? Where is your focus?
- Is it easy or difficult to trust in God's plan for your life? How does abiding in His presence help you?

For Further Reading: Mark 10:29-30, 1 Peter 5:10 and Romans 8:17-18

HOW TO RESPOND WHEN THINGS GO WRONG

Why, my soul, are you downcast? Why so disturbed within me? Put your hope in God, for I will yet praise Him, my Savior and my God.

—Psalm 42:11

Each challenge we face is an opportunity to cry out to God in prayer and supplication, lifting our hands in praise as Ephesians 4:6 states to the "one God and Father of all, who is over all and through all and in all."

James Stockdale was an American vice-admiral and a prisoner of war in North Vietnam. He wrote, "This is a very important lesson. You must never confuse faith that you will prevail in the end – which you cannot afford to lose – with the discipline to confront the most brutal facts of your current reality, whatever they might be."[1] This concept is known as the Stockdale Paradox, which is the paradox of simultaneously holding the "brutal facts of reality" and "faith," is one we all must learn to embrace.

Not long ago, I received news that my business had received yet another delay after seasons of decline. I was disappointed and felt self-pity enter my heart. After everything I had walked through over the last few years, this news left me very discouraged and, frankly, angry.

My home was gone.

My marriage was over.

My daughter had died.

I was experiencing other financial discouragements.

I felt pain and lack, and I was disgruntled because so many prophetic words given to me claimed my circumstances were on the upswing.

My response was to pour out my heart to God. I told Him in no uncertain terms how upset I was. (David did this all the time in the Psalms. It is healthy and important to let God know what we feel.) I vented and talked and vented some more. This continued on through the evening on my walk in the park nearby.

By the time I returned to my office, it had hit me that while I certainly could be upset about what was happening in a God-honouring way, there was an element of flesh involved in my response. Specifically, I had opened the door to self-pity, birthed from an attitude of entitlement. These attitudes dangerously paved the way to a depressive mindset and intense discouragement. As I gained clarity on what was going on inside of me, I took positive action, drawing on the instructions God gave us for such moments through the prophet, Isaiah.

> To proclaim the year of the Lord's favor and the day of vengeance of our God, to comfort all who mourn, and provide for those who grieve in Zion—to bestow on them a crown of beauty instead of ashes, the oil of joy instead of mourning, and a garment of praise instead of a spirit of despair. They will be called oaks of righteousness, a planting of the Lord for the display of his splendor.
>
> —Isaiah 61:2-3

The Holy Spirit guided me to understand that it was time to praise instead of wallow in the spirit of heaviness. With the help of a recorded praise session that I joined online, I lifted up my sacrifice of praise. I didn't want to. I didn't feel like praising... but I knew I had to. Miraculously, as I sang out the truth about the goodness of God, my heart slowly changed, and, ultimately, my peace was restored. We must never forget that it is not about what happens to us, but how we choose to respond to what happens to us that makes all the difference.

Invitation to Journey Deeper:

- How do you react or choose to respond to God when things go wrong?
- When things go wrong, and you feel frustrated or discouraged, what is the root of those emotions?
- How does the substance of faith factor into your suffering?

For Further Reading: Proverbs 3:5-6 and 2 Corinthians 1:4

---

1. Boris Groysberg and Robin Abrahams, "What the Stockdale Paradox Tells Us About Crisis Leadership," *Harvard Business School*, accessed February 14, 2021, https://hbswk.hbs.edu/item/what-the-stockdale-paradox-tells-us-about-crisis-leadership.

GIVING GLORY TO GOD

And I continually long to know the wonders of Jesus and to experi-
ence the overflowing power of His resurrection working in me. I will
be one with Him in His sufferings and become like Him in His death.

—Philippians 3:10, TPT

Suffering gives us an opportunity to glorify God. In it, we can willingly sacrifice ourselves and patiently endure whatever comes our way, knowing God is with us in our troubles. Our rational minds normally try to judge each situation according to what we think is good or evil, but the surrendered spirit knows His ways are higher than our ways. God simply asks us to obey, look to and trust Him, no matter the outcome. He is with us now, and He will be with us then, guiding and leading each of our steps. In this place, we find beautiful rest for our souls. We can trust the sovereign King of the universe and thank Him in every situation.

If something is worse than we imagined, praise Him!

If something is better than we thought, praise Him!

If a door closes, praise Him! When a door opens, praise Him!

When we feel like it, thank Him! When we don't feel like it, thank Him!

We must learn to praise God in all circumstances because God inhabits the praises of His people. I have learnt the answer to everything is *praise*. As we enter His gates with thanksgiving and His courts with praise, we will create healthy bonds to our Creator. (It is scientifically proven that we bond to the object of our gratitude and affection.)

Giving glory to God is a choice. Every day, we face opportunities to put God first. Sometimes it's easy, and we can't help but lift our hands in praise. Other times, praise feels like a discipline because things didn't go our way or we feel let down by life. *Remember: The works of the enemy should not impress us.* The enemy is like a roaring lion, but he is nothing compared to God! What the enemy intends for evil, God will use for good. His Word never returns void. It always accomplishes His purposes! As believers, we can walk in freedom, peace and union with the Father. In this way, we can actually live above our circumstances, paralyse the enemy, and allow God to use everything for our good.

So, choose to glorify God and never the enemy. When you focus on the problem, you make an idol of it. Suddenly, your struggle is bigger than God, and Satan has taken a foothold. Instead, choose to believe God is good, choose to trust and choose to praise Him in all circumstances. God knows the end from the beginning and has our eternal best interest in mind. Every choice we make for Jesus will produce eternal glory, more than we could ever imagine. Difficulties will arise, but believers are on the winning team of a war that is already won. Let us praise God in faith, for He is mighty to save and His promises never fail!

Invitation to Journey Deeper:

- Are you actively praising God in all circumstances, good and bad? What can you thank Him for right now?
- How can you incorporate praise and thanksgiving into your daily walk with God?

For Further Reading: 2 Corinthians 1:3, Zephaniah 3:17, Psalm 100:4, and Joshua 21:45

BREAKING AGREEMENTS

See to it that no one falls short of the grace of God and that no bitter root grows up to cause trouble and defile many.

—Hebrews 12:15

It doesn't matter how long you have been walking with Jesus; there is always more to learn and more ways to grow in your walk with God. There will be moments when our circumstances will challenge us to affirm our belief in God's goodness and sovereignty. There will be moments where the flesh tries to overpower our spirit. However, these opportunities give us a chance to crucify our flesh and be resurrected with Christ. When we are in the wilderness for a long time, we can lose gratitude and speak things out that do not agree with God's truth (as the Israelites did in the desert). In these moments, we need to repent for our attitude and response.

I remember one instance where I felt very angry and disappointed about how a situation at work had gone down. I spoke about what I was feeling with some mentors and prayer partners. Through the conversations, I realised I had opened the door to self-pity when I received the negative business report without God's grace. (Yes, there is theme here —entitlement rooted deep that the Lord was uprooting!) I allowed discouragement to enter my heart by partnering with a spirit of victimisation. I have experienced a lot of traumas since an early age, so it can be easy for me to use victim language when I talk about my life. This is exactly the trap I had allowed myself to fall into again. Because our words carry power, I was reaping the fruit of what I had spoken. I broke any agreement I had made with the enemy based on my words and attitudes, repented by changing my thinking and aligning my thoughts and mind with God, and declared God's truth over my life:

- *God has given me the authority to prosper in all I do.*

258

- *I am victorious in Jesus.*
- *I am not a victim.*
- *I will not be stolen from.*
- *I am highly favoured and greatly blessed.*
- *I am loved, and all is well within me because of Jesus.*
- *God is turning all things around.*
- *God has a better way, and I can expect an increase in the long run, not loss.*

In this story, more of my flesh needed the pruner's shears. But God is merciful and kind, and He is always ready to receive us when we return to Him. Sometimes you have to laugh at the schemes of the enemy. No matter what happens, God will ultimately restore and multiply. Whether now or in eternity, that is not our burden to carry. We are not working towards an earthly goal anyways! We are eternal beings working towards an eternal reward. We are not on an earthly clock! God desires for us to experience the freedom He offers, and it is available to us now.

Invitation to Journey Deeper:

- What has God already pruned in your life? Have you seen growth or maturity since that experience?
- Why is it difficult to break agreements with the enemy?
- Ask the Lord to search your heart and reveal to you any areas that need pruning. Repent of any agreements you have made with the enemy and declare God's truth over your life by writing them down and then reading them aloud.

For Further Reading: Mark 8:34

DISCIPLINE IN LOVE

Praise be to the God and Father of our Lord Jesus Christ, the Father of compassion and the God of all comfort, who comforts us in all our troubles, so that we can comfort those in any trouble with the comfort we ourselves receive from God.

—*2 Corinthians* 1:3-4

God is our perfect heavenly Father. Every lesson He teaches is for our own good (and the good of many others) and is multifaceted. Not only did the Lord reveal I embraced a victim mentality and how to deal with it, but He also revealed I had difficulty feeling compassion for victims or people struggling with an attitude or spirit of victimisation.

I was a hard-liner. I really thought that people just needed to *get over it* and stop being a victim… including myself. Eventually, the Lord opened my heart and eyes to the need for mercy to understand those who are suffering and see them as God sees them.

God is kind and gentle towards those in pain, including those suffering because of their own mistakes. He is compassionate towards us in our moments of weakness, and He asks us to be compassionate towards others and ourselves just the same. That doesn't mean He doesn't ask us to change or realign–He does. We experience the natural consequences of our choices, good and bad, and we learn from them. He wants what is best for us! He is a good Father who delights in His children!

> *The Lord your God is with you, the Mighty Warrior who saves. He will take great delight in you; in His love He will no longer rebuke you, but will rejoice over you with singing."*

—*Zephaniah* 3:17

However, sometimes that love looks like discipline, and occasionally, that discipline is painful. God disciplines those He loves like a good parent who corrects His son or daughter. Discipline helps us understand our faults and turns us from our wicked ways. It makes us more like Christ, who loves unconditionally, no matter where we are in our faith journey. He loves us at our best *and* at our worst.

Invitation to Journey Deeper:

- When have you experienced discipline in love? What was your perspective then versus your perspective of it now?
- Is it easy or difficult for you to have compassion for those who are struggling? Explain.
- How can you be more compassionate towards yourself or others who are struggling? Ask the Holy Spirit to help you see them as He does.

For Further Reading: Hebrews 12:6

PRESSING IN

The Lord is close to the brokenhearted and saves those who are crushed in spirit.

—Psalm 34:18

In pain, our temptation is to withdraw. When we press into painful experiences, we gain maturity that results in selfless love. As Proverbs 17:3 states, "The crucible for silver and the furnace for gold, but the Lord tests the heart." Learning to suffer well in the small, regular things ultimately builds trust. Seeing God come through with the little things builds faith, knowing He will come through with the big things.

David's confidence in God to rescue him from the giant Goliath is just one example of how faith grows through daily submission. When everyone else was afraid to battle Goliath, David was brave because he knew God was on His side. God was with him in the fields as he toiled alone. God was with him as he put his own life on the line for his sheep. And now, God would be with him as he fought the biggest giant he'd ever faced.

"The Lord who rescued me from the paw of the lion and the paw of the bear will rescue me from the hand of this Philistine."

Saul said to David, "Go, and the Lord be with you."

—1 Samuel 17:37

Perseverance, patient endurance, or longsuffering has been a consistent theme in my life. By the world's standards, I have every reason to be resentful, angry, and *damaged*. But that's not God's best. With every trouble and trauma, God has mourned with me. He has offered Himself as my source and strength to become more like Him as a testament to the hope He gives.

God is with us in our suffering. He is a loving Father who offers comfort in our distress. We are never alone in our pain. God *wants* us to call out to Him. Paul provides these encouraging words in 1 Peter 4:19 in *The Passion Translation*, which states, "So then, those who suffer for following God's will should enfold their lives into the Creator, who will never fail them, and continue to always do what is right."

Where the world is ever-changing, unstable, fickle, and built on shifting sand, God does not change. He is our rock, our ever-present help in times of need. Consider this praise from David:

> *God is our refuge and strength, an ever-present help in trouble.*
>
> —*Psalms 46:1*

Scripture reminds us over and over that we are not alone. The Lord is our strength and source, even in the worst of times... especially in the worst of times! When we are weak, He is strong.

Invitation to Journey Deeper:

- How is the Lord inviting you to *press in?*
- How or where do you need strength from the Lord today?

For Further Reading: James 4:8 and 1 Timothy 4:17

A GOOD WORK

For it has been granted to you on behalf of Christ not only to believe in Him, but also to suffer for Him.

—Philippians 1:29

Life is often difficult, and suffering is a fact of life. This is the reality of living in a fallen world. Knowing God can use suffering for our good enables us to keep our eyes on Him and not on ourselves. As we pick up our cross and follow Jesus, suffering becomes a crucifixion of our old, selfish nature. In time, we learn to receive the revelation of our completeness in Him. With it comes joy everlasting!

Those the LORD has rescued will return. They will enter Zion with singing; everlasting joy will crown their heads.

—Isaiah 51:11a

Our attitude while suffering gives glory to either God or Satan, and we get to choose whom we glorify. Many times, physical health and financial prosperity lull us into a place of comfort, complacency, and, worse, self-sufficiency and entitlement. God knows what we need and what is best for us in His divine timing. The happiness and joy we find on earth may be momentarily satisfying, but the peace that comes from God is eternal!

In my life, the high degree of financial shaking and personal grief, much of it due to my own making, taught me that money is not the ultimate source of security. God ultimately used my trials and suffering for my good. I wouldn't have the freedom I have today had I not gone through the fiery furnace. With God as my foundation and source of security, the pressure is off, although the Lord continues to test and refine me!

When I feel burdened, it's a sign that I am relying on my ability (pride), and I quickly pass it over to God. When a business deal goes south or relationships fail me, I know God will provide a new way forward. All I have to do is receive His peace and rely on His power.

Moving in the Spirit allows us to see past our circumstances and trust that God is doing a good work—and He will finish what He started. This is how believers can experience contentment and joy and rejoice, even while in prison or in times of extreme affliction.

Your suffering does not have to own you or prevent you from experiencing the goodness of God. Suffering is an invitation to greater intimacy, to rest in His presence, and to share in His glory!

Our struggles do not have to take us down. With our eyes pointed towards the One who saves, suffering can refine us, making us more like Him as we participate in the work of the cross.

Invitation to Journey Deeper:

- When have you experienced a "shaking" that ultimately produced a good work?
- When have you let your suffering prevent you from experiencing the goodness of God?
- Why is it easy to find comfort in worldly things?

For Further Reading: Philippians 1:6

THERE IS HOPE

Even though I walk through the darkest valley, I will fear no evil, for You are with me; Your rod and Your staff, they comfort me.

—Psalm 23:4

A friend of mine uses the term "the Armed Shepherd" to describe the safety Jesus provides. True comfort comes only with both the rod and the staff. Confrontation and discipline, the rod, transforms and delivers us from sin while the staff provides safety and security. We need to embrace the entire scripture.

God's Word has been my hope and my anchor as I have endured suffering. Both Job and David suffered acutely and saw God restore their lives in powerful ways. Thousands of years later, God is still making all things work together for good.

My suffering has transformed me into an overcomer. Tests produce testimonies. My story can now strengthen and encourage others. It is our attitude as we endure suffering that brings glory to God. I know I have not always been patient in my suffering, but I have endured. Endurance results from the knowledge of God's goodness, faithfulness, and sovereignty, knowing His grace is always sufficient. It is our sovereign God who oversees every aspect of our lives as we are in Him. Trust in Him!

Jeanne Guyon was a Christian from the 1600s who went through intense persecution, illness, and imprisonment for her beliefs in Jesus. She was well acquainted with suffering and experienced the deep impact of developing spiritual maturity through death to self and growing in intimacy with God. In her book, *Intimacy in Christ*, she wrote,

"Do not insult the work of the cross by complaining about your problems. Welcome trials, for they teach you what you are and lead you to renounce yourself and yourself is, of all possessions, the most dangerous... All that should concern you is glorifying God."[1]

I know that my suffering is nothing compared to the suffering of Jesus. He paid the full price, suffering to the extreme mentally, emotionally, physically, and spiritually. On earth, what looked like the greatest defeat was actually the greatest victory for all of eternity. Unimaginable suffering. Unimaginable victory! His hope is available to all, a glorious inheritance for all who call Him Lord.

Invitation to Journey Deeper:

- Are you an overcomer or a victim of your suffering?[2]
- What gives you hope that there is more beyond this earthly suffering?
- Is there a story, passage, or person in the Bible who encourages you? How so?

For Further Reading: 1 Corinthians 11:1

---

1. Jeanne Guyon, *Intimacy in Christ, Her Letters Now in Modern English* (Seedsowers, 1989).
2. I highly recommend reading my daughter Bryn's chapter "Victim vs. Victor Mindset" in her book *Dying to Live*, page 165.

PURPOSE IN OUR PAIN

And I will ask the Father, and He will give you another advocate to help you and be with you forever—the Spirit of truth. The world cannot accept Him, because it neither sees Him nor knows Him. But you know Him, for He lives with you and will be in you.

—John 14:16-17

In our tragedies and in our pain, God encounters us. Just before His crucifixion, Jesus told the disciples that He would ask the Father to send an advocate: the Holy Spirit. We have access to the same Holy Spirit! He is with us constantly to guide us, advocate for us, and to be with us as we walk this earth every day. He does not leave us to fend for ourselves. He has given us a helper who will never leave us.

God also gives us a promise to cling to in the midst of our suffering in Matthew 6:33, "But seek first His Kingdom and His righteousness, and all these things will be given to you as well." As we seek after God's heart and make Him and His will our focus, He will give us the desires of our heart because they align with His. My testimony alone is evidence of this and gives me the ability to walk others through hard seasons and point them back to God.

When we overcome and walk in freedom despite our circumstances or our pasts through the power of the Holy Spirit, God anoints us to encourage others facing similar trials. Allowing God to redeem our pain for the sake of others is an incredible aspect of redemption.

Through suffering and pain, I have persevered and overcome many things. I have grown in faith and grown in surrender. I have an incredible history with God. He has proven His goodness and faithfulness in my life. In fact, these pages are a result of wanting to share what the Lord has done to transform the pain in my life and family into my purpose. I long for you to experience the same freedom in your life.

Today, God continues to give me opportunities to care for others who are facing enormous trials. I hope by now you can see through my story that Jesus redeems everything and uses everything for our good. What He did for me He offers to you. This is the testimony of Jesus, the Spirit of Prophecy! Your pain is not wasted when submitted to Jesus. Through patience and faith, we inherit God's promise.

Invitation to Journey Deeper:

- Do you feel alone in your suffering? Why or why not?
- How does it feel to know that you have someone (the Holy Spirit) sent specifically to help you and be your advocate?
- How have you seen your past suffering used for good?
- Is there something in your past that you can use for the glory of God? Pause and ask God to show you how to use your past hurts for good.

For Further Reading: John 14:16-17 and Psalm 37:4

THE BLESSING OF HOLDING ON

And the God of all grace, who called you to His eternal glory in Christ, after you have suffered a little while, will Himself restore you and make you strong, firm and steadfast. To Him be the power for ever and ever. Amen.

—1 Peter 5:10-11

If you're in a season of suffering, I feel for you. It is not an easy season to be in, but it can become such a season of blessing if you press into God. It is important not to fall into the rut of self-pity. Cry out to God, as Job did. As David did. As Paul did. As Jesus did. Lean on other believers for support. Breaking and crushing are a step on the journey to new life and freedom. They are not the destination. When we get stuck in the crushing, we lose sight of our purpose.

For many, suffering can become a source of comfort because it is familiar. We get used to the pity of others, or we question if making different choices will actually result in a different outcome. The world is out to get us, and the work it takes to leave our old selves behind often seems too big a task to bear.

When we indulge in our suffering, choosing to stay in it instead of giving everything over to God, we become victims of our circumstances. When we submit everything to God, trusting in His will and His ways, He will personally and powerfully restore us. He will build us up. He has all the power to do it! His grace is sufficient for anything that comes our way.

While God is sovereign and nothing happens without His permission, let me be very clear that God does not seek for us to suffer so we can "earn" our way to becoming more mature (although that is often the result). Our loving Father is working all things together for our good because *He is good!*

Joy is not the absence of suffering, but the presence of God.

—Janet Erskine Stuart[1]

Job's story ends with being blessed two-fold. His siblings comfort and console him by bringing gifts of gold and silver. God fills his land with animals and his home with children. He lives to see his great-grandchildren—an old man of 140 years.

No blessing on earth will compare to the riches of sharing in eternal glory with Christ. But I can promise you this... experiencing His presence in life's storms and tragedies is worth every sacrifice. Suffering is temporary—glory with Jesus is eternal.

Invitation to Journey Deeper:

- Are you stuck in a season of crushing? What is keeping you from experiencing God's goodness?
- Have you found false comfort in your pain? What of God's grace is He inviting you to experience through this process?

For Further Reading: Job 42:16

———————————————————

1. Elisabeth Elliot, "Elisabeth Elliot: 'Your Suffering Is Never for Nothing,'" *The Gospel Coalition*, accessed February 19, 2022, https://www.thegospelcoalition.org/article/elisabeth-elliot-suffering-never-nothing/.

AN ETERNAL PERSPECTIVE

He will wipe every tear from their eyes. There will be no more death or mourning or crying or pain, for the old order of things has passed away.

—Revelation 21:4

As I write these words, my daughter's murder case is coming to a close.

It has been difficult hearing all the incredibly gory details once again. However, my prayer is that Abbe's death will have a great impact on eternity and that all those involved will choose salvation. I am agreeing with God's will as stated in 2 Peter 3:9, "The Lord is not slow in keeping His promise, as some understand slowness. Instead He is patient with you, not wanting anyone to perish, but for everyone to come to repentance."

If we could see from heaven's perspective, we would join the Lord as He sits on His throne, laughing at the schemes of the enemy. He knows the eternal outcome for Satan (who is defeated already). We are like mist in the air, here for a little while, then gone. Our treasure is in heaven. It's important to keep our eyes on the prize. This is why in 2 Corinthians 4:17, Paul called having his feet smashed with steel rods, being beaten and imprisoned multiple times, etc., "...light and momentary troubles..." Paul knew his suffering was producing an eternal weight of glory beyond all comparison.

Proper perspective changes everything! In reality, what we see ahead of us is likely just a tiny thread of God's great tapestry. It might even be a dark thread that seems daunting and impossibly bleak. But it's those dark threads woven in that often highlight the good things God is doing. All threads serve a purpose and only God can see the fulness of the His masterpiece under construction. We can rest assured no matter what happens on earth; our true treasure is in heaven. Now that is an incredible investment and trade-off!

When you go through intense suffering with someone you love, you grow closer to them. In the same way, suffering with God produces greater levels of intimacy. Hearing of the dark world Abbe lived in was painful, but I felt God's presence with me through each wave of sadness. In such moments of unbelievable anguish, we get to understand the true meaning of Emmanuel, God with us. We get to receive the tangible *shalom* of Jesus when the world is falling apart. Miraculously, He helped me remain in peace and trust. I forgave Abbe's murderers long ago; there is no hold of bitterness on my heart or mind.

I am thankful for the sweet memories and gifts of Abbe's short life. There are still times of tears, but they are filled with love for Abbe and gratitude for God's mercy and eternal life and the freedom Abbe is now experiencing. My younger daughter, Bryn, and I are looking forward to a day when we can share the gospel with Abbe's murderers. We both know that Jesus can redeem anything. We hold on to God's promises and trust in His resurrection power.

Invitation to Journey Deeper:

- How has your view of suffering changed over the course of these reflections?
- In what ways could your pain be redeemed by allowing Jesus into your suffering?

For Further Reading: James 4:14, Hebrews 10:34-35, Acts 14:19; 16:23 and 2 Corinthians 11:25

THE GOSPEL OF THE KINGDOM OF GOD

The Spirit of the Lord is on me, because He has anointed me to proclaim good news to the poor. He has sent me to proclaim freedom for the prisoners and recovery of sight for the blind, to set the oppressed free, to proclaim the year of the Lord's favor.

— Luke 4:18-19

Salvation (being born again) is just the inception point of the journey with Jesus although, sadly, many Christians stall at this point because the gospel of the Kingdom has not been preached.

Jesus preached the gospel of the Kingdom of God and Jesus is the door into His Kingdom. His blood paid the price and established the new covenant. You have moved from the kingdom of this world (darkness) to the Kingdom of God. You are in the world but no longer of the world.

Jesus began His public ministry with the words, "Repent, for the Kingdom of God is at hand."

To repent is to turn away from sin and toward Jesus. Ultimately, repentance leads to changing the way we think which changes the way we behave. Jesus came to bring the news that His Kingdom has arrived. It is Jesus who rules over the Kingdom of God which will radically change everything in your life. The Kingdom of God has come to earth once again and we have been restored as children of God, recovering all that was lost in Adam. As God originally intended before the fall, we can once again assume dominion to rule and reign as ambassadors of Jesus on the earth, citizens of the Kingdom of God. We are now God's family, sons and daughters and heirs of Jesus, the King of kings, *royalty*.

Just like Jesus, we are to proclaim the gospel of the Kingdom of God which is far beyond salvation. This is the Kingdom ruled by God and, as His sons and daughters, we have legal rights, privileges and responsibilities as ambassadors of His government. This is our inheritance as citizens of heaven, His Kingdom that was prepared for us and lost in the fall, restored on the earth.

We must remember, "the earth is the Lord's, the fulness thereof, and all that dwell within it." The earth is His already so there is nothing to conquer as in traditional kingdom invasions and expansions of physical territory. God also set up the earth to work through people when He said "let them have dominion over...all the earth," transferring His authority to man. This is why God must partner with us to bring heaven to earth and we empower God to move through prayer.

The mission of Jesus is about transforming hearts and minds to establish His Kingdom within the hearts of people. This is how God establishes His Kingdom from the invisible realm into the physical realm. We have access to His Kingdom to fulfill our destiny on the earth.

The Bible is the constitution of God's Kingdom. His Word is law. His will is absolute as He is King. We are to know the will of the King and carry out His will on earth as it is in heaven just as Jesus did by only doing what He saw the Father doing and saying what He heard the Father saying. There is a maturity process, renewing our minds to this Kingdom reality so we can live rightly, surrendering to the power of the Holy Spirit to flow through us. This is the Kingdom of Heaven, where God's Kingdom has full authority, in and through us, on earth as it is in heaven.

Transformed people transform people. When the Kingdom of God has taken over our hearts, it allows us to bring the Kingdom of Heaven to our families, workplaces, church, neighborhoods, and our spheres of influence. It is an entirely new way of life, coming back to original intent, to exercise dominion and authority over the earth under the Kingship of Jesus. We have been reestablished as rulers (stewardship not ownership) over the physical realm.

We are not in a holding pattern awaiting to die to go to heaven, rather we get to enter into the Kingdom of God on earth as Kingdom citizens. This is our mission and call on earth, to proclaim the good news of the Kingdom of God as the Lord has already empowered and equipped us to do through the power of the Holy Spirit.

Invitation to Journey Deeper:

- Are you following the mission of Jesus to preach the gospel of the Kingdom? What step can you take in alignment with this call on your life?
- How does this perspective on the gospel change the way you look at Christianity?

For Further Reading: Genesis 1:26, ESV Matthew 4:17, and Psalm 24:1

Epilogue

The precepts of the Lord are right, giving joy to the heart.

The commands of the Lord are radiant, giving light to the eyes. The fear of the Lord is pure, enduring forever.

The decrees of the Lord are firm, and all of them are righteous.

They are more precious than gold, than much pure gold; they are sweeter than honey, than honey from the honeycomb.

—Psalm 19:8-10

The gospel tells us of God's love and forgiveness. Accepting the truth of the gospel through faith in Jesus paves the way for us to live as we were created to be, with nothing to hide, unafraid to tell the truth. My story is one that displays the redemptive power of the gospel.

As this book draws to a close, I hope you have learnt something from my journey with the Lord. It hasn't always been straightforward, and I have made a multitude of mistakes along the way. But, through it all, God has guided me and transformed me more than I could have ever imagined—and I know His work is not finished! The more I lean into Him, the more time I spend in His presence and submit to His ways, the more my life and my ways reflect Him.

Our lives are living epistles, or "living letters." Your story likely looks different from mine, but I am confident God wants to redeem it just the same. He desperately wants us to experience life with Him! That life, I can assure you, is better than any comfort this world has given me. But there is a cost. Experiencing His glorious freedom requires our submission and trust. It means giving up the sin we are entangled in (which often satisfies our flesh). It asks us to die to ourselves, being co-crucified with Christ so that we are slaves no longer.

Jesus came as a man so that we could see what is possible if we allow God to work through us in His grace. Jesus gave Himself as the final sacrifice for a world more consumed with itself than its Creator. The hope He offers separates us from our pride and unites us with Him once again. The best news is that we don't have to do it alone. We *can't* do it alone. God meets us exactly where we are and promises to comfort us, protect us, and guide us. No matter how far off the path we veer, He will always come to find us! Like a good shepherd, Jesus is faithful to find His lost sheep and celebrate its return.

> I tell you that in the same way there will be more rejoicing in heaven over one sinner who repents than over ninety-nine righteous persons who do not need to repent.
>
> —Luke 15:7

God's goodness is beyond comprehension and is limitless. His goodness never changes. Knowing this is foundational to our faith and our anchor in times of trouble! God in His goodness came after me. Despite meeting the Lord at a young age, I veered far off the path. Although my intentions were often good, my motives were wrong. I thought I could fix most things with money or good deeds. In reality, my spirit was tormented, and the solace I found in the world only made things worse.

Giving my life over to God in 2016 was the beginning of something new for me. Much change would happen in the years to come, but making the choice to follow Him was the catalyst for transformation that needed to happen in my life. I grieved much loss at first. Letting go of what you've always known can be difficult. Though God was breaking chains and releasing me from the grip of the enemy, I still mourned what was. Even positive change can be difficult!

God showed up in my pain. He showed up in my brokenness. He healed old wounds and reminded me who He created me to be—His child, a son of God. And in the midst of one of the greatest tragedies of my life, the death of my daughter Abbe and the near loss of her sister, Bryn, in the aftermath, God gave me overwhelming peace. A peace that still comforts me today as I face the fiery trials that life still brings. I have experienced the redemptive power of the gospel in so many tangible ways. As the Prince of Peace pursues me and I submit to His Lordship, God makes me more like Him every day. That is the process of sanctification. As He is holy and set apart, so too am I! I am made blameless through the blood of Christ.

The more we abide in God's presence and listen to His voice, the more transformation we will experience. By repenting, surrendering, and choosing to walk with our eyes fixed on Jesus, we mature spiritually. God gives us many tools to help us along the way: the Bible, the church community, mentors and spiritual leaders, the Holy Spirit, spiritual gifts, dreams, spiritual armour, and so much more.

As Christians, we learn to apply the victory of Jesus to every area of our lives, moving into the fulness of our new creation life, in union with Him. As we mature, we move into our God-given purpose to worship Him and are enabled to steward our inheritance, bringing heaven to earth. Our freedom is not only for our benefit but so that we might point others back to Jesus. May we not hide the treasure that we hold inside but let His light shine through the cracks of our broken vessels.

To continue this journey of maturing together, I encourage you to connect with M46 Ministries. I also encourage you to read Bryn's beautiful autobiography, *Dying to Live*, written in the aftermath of Abbe's death. It recounts not only Bryn's journey to cross, but her healing that resulted from abiding at the feet of Jesus. As of writing this epilogue, my mother, Bryn, and I are preparing to write our story of family healing.

I hope that you have tasted and seen the Lord's goodness through my story and the transformation both Bryn and I have experienced. I assure you He has a feast of freedom for you to enjoy! What God did for me and Bryn, He will do for you! God shows no favoritism and loves us all the same. That said, your journey will look different than ours. We are all unique and will uniquely experience God's hand in our lives. We cannot compare our journey to anyone else's. God knows what we need, when we need it. He meets us wherever we are at.

As always, God loves you and is here for you. He is the Alpha and Omega. The beginning and the end. He makes all things work together for our good. He is our comforter and great hope. You are never, ever alone. He is already standing in your future with open arms. He is ready for you to embrace Him and live out the good works that He prepared in advance for you!

The Lord bless you and keep you; the Lord make His face shine on you and be gracious to you; the Lord turn His face toward you and give you peace.

—*Numbers 6:24-26*

God is good!

Blessings,
Bryan Elliott

Spiritual Maturity

ASSESSMENT

Checking In

You are now finished with the first book in the *More Than Gold* collection! It's a great time to check in to see how you have grown spiritually and consider any areas that need attention. Remember, spiritual growth is a journey! God loves you as you are and is excited to be on the journey with you. All He wants is your time and focus.

"Remain in Me, as I also remain in you. No branch can bear fruit by itself; it must remain in the vine. Neither can you bear fruit unless you remain in Me." -John 15:4

Read through the list of words below, filling in the bubble you feel best represents your level of spiritual maturity. Be honest with yourself, asking God to give you clarity about the condition of your heart. This is not a test, but rather an opportunity to evaluate your walk with God and an encouragement to pursue greater intimacy with Him!

SPIRITUAL MATURITY ASSESSMENT

Selfish Love (Worldly)	1	2	3	4	5	6	7	8	9	10	Sacrificial Love (Gospel)

Selfish Love (Worldly) ○—○—○—○—○—○—○—○—○—○ Sacrificial Love (Gospel)
1   2   3   4   5   6   7   8   9   10

Prideful ○—○—○—○—○—○—○—○—○—○ Humble
1   2   3   4   5   6   7   8   9   10

Tormented ○—○—○—○—○—○—○—○—○—○ Peaceful
1   2   3   4   5   6   7   8   9   10

Bitter ○—○—○—○—○—○—○—○—○—○ Merciful
1   2   3   4   5   6   7   8   9   10

Wounded ○—○—○—○—○—○—○—○—○—○ Healed
1   2   3   4   5   6   7   8   9   10

Religious (Law) ○—○—○—○—○—○—○—○—○—○ Relational (Grace)
1   2   3   4   5   6   7   8   9   10

Victim Mindset ○—○—○—○—○—○—○—○—○—○ Overcomer
1   2   3   4   5   6   7   8   9   10

Hopeless ○—○—○—○—○—○—○—○—○—○ Hope Filled
1   2   3   4   5   6   7   8   9   10

Depressed ○—○—○—○—○—○—○—○—○—○ Joy Filled
1   2   3   4   5   6   7   8   9   10

Fearful ○—○—○—○—○—○—○—○—○—○ Courageous
1   2   3   4   5   6   7   8   9   10

Condemned ○—○—○—○—○—○—○—○—○—○ Innocent
1   2   3   4   5   6   7   8   9   10

Self-Focus ○—○—○—○—○—○—○—○—○—○ Kingdom-Focus
1   2   3   4   5   6   7   8   9   10

SPIRITUAL MATURITY ASSESSMENT

	1	2	3	4	5	6	7	8	9	10	
Impulsive	○	○	○	○	○	○	○	○	○	○	Self-Controlled
Stingy	○	○	○	○	○	○	○	○	○	○	Generous
Prayerless	○	○	○	○	○	○	○	○	○	○	Prayerful
Easily Offended	○	○	○	○	○	○	○	○	○	○	Gracious
Impatient	○	○	○	○	○	○	○	○	○	○	Patient
Unforgiving	○	○	○	○	○	○	○	○	○	○	Forgiving
Control	○	○	○	○	○	○	○	○	○	○	Surrender
Unsatisfied	○	○	○	○	○	○	○	○	○	○	Content
Lukewarm	○	○	○	○	○	○	○	○	○	○	Passionate
Disconnected	○	○	○	○	○	○	○	○	○	○	Intimacy with God & People
Self-Reliant	○	○	○	○	○	○	○	○	○	○	God-Dependent
Know God Is Father	○	○	○	○	○	○	○	○	○	○	Know God As Father

After going through the list, look back at the spiritual assessment you filled out at the beginning of this book. How do your answers compare now? In which areas have you grown? What areas need attention? Are there areas you are struggling in that you weren't before? As you look forward, how would you like to grow in the next year? What are some tangible steps you can take on your spiritual growth journey?

Take some time to journal through these questions and reflect on your spiritual life and walk with God. Remember, He is with you and He is for you... every step of the way. For a more extensive version of this assessment and additional resources, visit m46ministries.com/extras. Consider inviting others on the journey with you by reviewing the assessment results together. Trusted believers can help us spot blind spots and discover new areas of growth. God did not design us to walk this life alone, but in a community of believers who will encourage us and point us to Jesus daily.

DYING
TO
LIVE

Experiencing
God's Redemptive
Power in the Midst
of Tragedy

Bryn S. Elliott

Dying to Live is the captivating true story of Bryn Elliott, whose life was marked by trauma, abuse, addiction, rape, rebellion, and the tragic murder of her older sister, Abbe. Once hopeless, alone, and wishing for death, Bryn candidly shares her journey of overcoming the enemy to experience a life transformed by the Savior.

Today, Bryn's testimony declares God's love to a generation marked by depression, addiction, and a total loss of identity. Her story shines light on the darkness and gives hope to the weary. For those who have struggled with addiction, abuse, and severe personal loss, Bryn's experience gives purpose to their pain.

This two-part book invites readers into the most vulnerable parts of a daughter's journey to freedom, and then offers practical insight, wisdom, tools, and encouragement toward an intimate relationship with Jesus. A surrendered life might not always be easy, but it will always be worth it.

> *"THIS BOOK IS A PROFOUND, EVEN SACRED MASTERPIECE. IT HAS LEFT ME BREATHLESS WITH WONDER AND AWE IN CELEBRATION OF THE GOODNESS OF GOD'S OUTRAGEOUS LOVE."*
> **-MICHELE OKIMURA** EXECUTIVE DIRECTOR, EXPLICIT MOVEMENT

www.M46Ministries.com

BE THE FIRST TO KNOW

Continue your journey through the *More than Gold* series with Bryan Elliott's second book

COMING SOON!

Greater than Silver is a collection of reflections designed to deepen your roots in Christ. One day, one step at a time through the power of the Holy Spirit, you can strengthen your faith and grow into a mature believer ready to walk out the fullness of God's call in your life.

M46MINISTRIES.COM

A BETTER WAY

Made in the USA
Monee, IL
02 July 2023

38140813R00177